MznLnx

Missing Links Exam Preps

Exam Prep for

Intermediate Algebra

Martin-Gay, 3rd Edition

The MznLnx Exam Prep is your link from the texbook and lecture to your exams.
The MznLnx Exam Preps are unauthorized and comprehensive reviews of your textbooks.

All material provided by MznLnx and Rico Publications (c) 2010
Textbook publishers and textbook authors do not particpate in or contribute to these reviews.

MznLnx

Rico
Publications

Exam Prep for Intermediate Algebra
3rd Edition
Martin-Gay

Publisher: Raymond Houge
Assistant Editor: Michael Rouger
Text and Cover Designer: Lisa Buckner
Marketing Manager: Sara Swagger
Project Manager, Editorial Production: Jerry Emerson
Art Director: Vernon Lowerui

Product Manager: Dave Mason
Editorial Assitant: Rachel Guzmanji
Pedagogy: Debra Long
Cover Image: Jim Reed/Getty Images
Text and Cover Printer: City Printing, Inc.
Compositor: Media Mix, Inc.

(c) 2010 Rico Publications
ALL RIGHTS RESERVED. No part of this work covered by the copyright may be reproduced or used in any form or by an means--graphic, electronic, or mechanical, including photocopying, recording, taping, Web distribution, information storage, and retrieval systems, or in any other manner--without the written permission of the publisher.

Printed in the United States
ISBN:

For more information about our products, contact us at:
Dave.Mason@RicoPublications.com

For permission to use material from this text or product, submit a request online to:
Dave.Mason@RicoPublications.com

Contents

CHAPTER 1
REAL NUMBERS AND ALGEBRAIC EXPRESSIONS — 1

CHAPTER 2
EQUATIONS, INEQUALITIES, AND PROBLEM SOLVING — 14

CHAPTER 3
GRAPHS AND FUNCTIONS — 29

CHAPTER 4
SYSTEMS OF EQUATIONS — 41

CHAPTER 5
EXPONENTS, POLYNOMIALS, AND POLYNOMIAL FUNCTIONS — 52

CHAPTER 6
RATIONAL EXPRESSIONS — 68

CHAPTER 7
RATIONAL EXPONENTS, RADICALS, AND COMPLEX NUMBERS — 84

CHAPTER 8
QUADRATIC EQUATIONS AND FUNCTIONS — 98

CHAPTER 9
CONIC SECTIONS — 112

CHAPTER 10
EXPONENTIAL AND LOGARITHMIC FUNCTIONS — 123

CHAPTER 11
SEQUENCES, SERIES, AND THE BINOMIAL THEOREM — 125

ANSWER KEY — 127

TO THE STUDENT

COMPREHENSIVE

The *MznLnx* Exam Prep series is designed to help you pass your exams. Editors at MznLnx review your textbooks and then prepare these practice exams to help you master the textbook material. Unlike study guides, workbooks, and practice tests provided by the texbook publisher and textbook authors, *MznLnx* gives you **all** of the material in each chapter in exam form, not just samples, so you can be sure to nail your exam.

MECHANICAL

The MznLnx Exam Prep series creates exams that will help you learn the subject matter as well as test you on your understanding. Each question is designed to help you master the concept. Just working through the exams, you gain an understanding of the subject--its a simple mechanical process that produces success.

INTEGRATED STUDY GUIDE AND REVIEW

MznLnx is not just a set of exams designed to test you, its also a comprehensive review of the subject content. Each exam question is also a review of the concept, making sure that you will get the answer correct without having to go to other sources of material. You learn as you go! Its the easiest way to pass an exam.

HUMOR

Studying can be tedious and dry. MznLnx's instructional design includes moderate humor within the exam questions on occassion, to break the tedium and revitalize the brain

Chapter 1. REAL NUMBERS AND ALGEBRAIC EXPRESSIONS

1. In mathematics, a _____ may be described informally as a number that can be given by an infinite decimal representation.
   a. Real number0
   b. Thing
   c. Undefined
   d. Undefined

2. _____ or arithmetics is the oldest and most elementary branch of mathematics, used by almost everyone, for tasks ranging from simple daily counting to advanced science and business calculations.
   a. Arithmetic0
   b. Thing
   c. Undefined
   d. Undefined

3. An _____ is a combination of numbers, operators, grouping symbols and/or free variables and bound variables arranged in a meaningful way which can be evaluated..
   a. Expression0
   b. Thing
   c. Undefined
   d. Undefined

4. In mathematics, a _____ of a complex-valued function f is a member x of the domain of f such that f(x) vanishes at x, that is, $x : f(x) = 0$.
   a. Thing
   b. Root0
   c. Undefined
   d. Undefined

5. _____ has many meanings, most of which simply .
   a. Thing
   b. Power0
   c. Undefined
   d. Undefined

6. A _____ is a symbolic representation denoting a quantity or expression. It often represents an "unknown" quantity that has the potential to change.
   a. Thing
   b. Variable0
   c. Undefined
   d. Undefined

7. _____ is a branch of mathematics concerning the study of structure, relation and quantity.
   a. Concept
   b. Algebra0
   c. Undefined
   d. Undefined

8. _____ forms part of thinking. Considered the most complex of all intellectual functions, _____ has been defined as higher-order cognitive process that requires the modulation and control of more routine or fundamental skills.
   a. Problem solving0
   b. Thing
   c. Undefined
   d. Undefined

9. In business, particularly accounting, a _____ is the time intervals that the accounts, statement, payments, or other calculations cover.
   a. Thing
   b. Period0
   c. Undefined
   d. Undefined

10. A _____ is a negotiable instrument instructing a financial institution to pay a specific amount of a specific currency from a specific demand account held in the maker/depositor's name with that institution. Both the maker and payee may be natural persons or legal entities.

Chapter 1. REAL NUMBERS AND ALGEBRAIC EXPRESSIONS

    a. Check0   b. Thing
    c. Undefined   d. Undefined

11. Acid _____ ratio measures the ability of a company to use its near cash or quick assets to immediately extinguish its current liabilities.
    a. Thing   b. Test0
    c. Undefined   d. Undefined

12. A frame of _____ is a particular perspective from which the universe is observed.
    a. Thing   b. Reference0
    c. Undefined   d. Undefined

13. The _____, the average in everyday English, which is also called the arithmetic _____ (and is distinguished from the geometric _____ or harmonic _____). The average is also called the sample _____. The expected value of a random variable, which is also called the population _____.
    a. Thing   b. Mean0
    c. Undefined   d. Undefined

14. In geometry, the _____ of an object is a point in some sense in the middle of the object.
    a. Thing   b. Center0
    c. Undefined   d. Undefined

15. In set theory and its applications throughout mathematics, _____ are a collection of sets (or sometimes other mathematical objects) that can be unambiguously defined by a property that all its members share.
    a. Classes0   b. Thing
    c. Undefined   d. Undefined

16. In economics, supply and _____ describe market relations between prospective sellers and buyers of a good.
    a. Demand0   b. Thing
    c. Undefined   d. Undefined

17. In mathematics, a _____ function in the sense of algebraic geometry is an everywhere-defined, polynomial function on an algebraic variety V with values in the field K over which V is defined.
    a. Regular0   b. Thing
    c. Undefined   d. Undefined

18. In mathematics, a _____ can mean either an element of the set {1, 2, 3, ...} (i.e the positive integers or the counting numbers) or an element of the set {0, 1, 2, 3, ...} (i.e. the non-negative integers).
    a. Natural number0   b. Thing
    c. Undefined   d. Undefined

19. In mathematics, a _____ number is a number which can be expressed as a ratio of two integers. Non-integer _____ numbers (commonly called fractions) are usually written as the vulgar fraction a / b, where b is not zero.
    a. Thing   b. Rational0
    c. Undefined   d. Undefined

Chapter 1. REAL NUMBERS AND ALGEBRAIC EXPRESSIONS

20. In mathematics, a _____ can mean either an element of the set {1, 2, 3, ...} (i.e the positive integers) or an element of the set {0, 1, 2, 3, ...} (i.e. the non-negative integers).
    a. Concept
    b. Whole number0
    c. Undefined
    d. Undefined

21. The _____ are the only integral domain whose positive elements are well-ordered, and in which order is preserved by addition. Like the natural numbers, the _____ form a countably infinite set. The set of all _____ is usually denoted in mathematics by a boldface Z .
    a. Thing
    b. Integers0
    c. Undefined
    d. Undefined

22. In mathematics, an _____ number is any real number that is not a rational number- that is, it is a number which cannot be expressed as a fraction m/n, where m and n are integers.
    a. Thing
    b. Irrational0
    c. Undefined
    d. Undefined

23. In mathematics, _____ is an elementary arithmetic operation. When one of the numbers is a whole number, _____ is the repeated sum of the other number.
    a. Multiplication0
    b. Thing
    c. Undefined
    d. Undefined

24. In elementary algebra, an _____ is a set that contains every real number between two indicated numbers and may contain the two numbers themselves.
    a. Interval0
    b. Thing
    c. Undefined
    d. Undefined

25. A _____ is a four-sided plane figure that has two sets of opposite parallel sides.
    a. Concept
    b. Parallelogram0
    c. Undefined
    d. Undefined

26. _____ are the basic objects of study in graph theory. Informally speaking, a graph is a set of objects called points, nodes, or vertices connected by links called lines or edges.
    a. Thing
    b. Graphs0
    c. Undefined
    d. Undefined

27. A _____ is a one-dimensional picture in which the integers are shown as specially-marked points evenly spaced on a line.
    a. Number line0
    b. Thing
    c. Undefined
    d. Undefined

28. In mathematics, the _____ of a coordinate system is the point where the axes of the system intersect.
    a. Origin0
    b. Thing
    c. Undefined
    d. Undefined

29. A _____ is a number that is less than zero.

Chapter 1. REAL NUMBERS AND ALGEBRAIC EXPRESSIONS

    a. Negative number0   b. Thing
    c. Undefined   d. Undefined

30. _____ (plural ellipses; from Greek ἔλλειψις 'omission') in linguistics refers to any omitted part of speech that is understood; i.e. the omission is intentional.
    a. Ellipsis0   b. Concept
    c. Undefined   d. Undefined

31. Mathematical _____ is used to represent ideas.
    a. Notation0   b. Thing
    c. Undefined   d. Undefined

32. An _____ or member of a set is an object that when collected together make up the set.
    a. Thing   b. Element0
    c. Undefined   d. Undefined

33. In mathematics, the _____, or members of a set or more generally a class are all those objects which when collected together make up the set or class.
    a. Thing   b. Elements0
    c. Undefined   d. Undefined

34. In mathematics and more specifically set theory, the _____ set is the unique set which contains no elements.
    a. Thing   b. Empty0
    c. Undefined   d. Undefined

35. In measure theory, a _____ is a set that is negligible for the purposes of the measure in question.
    a. Null set0   b. Concept
    c. Undefined   d. Undefined

36. In mathematics, an inequality is a statement about the relative size or order of two objects. For example 14 > 10, or 14 is _____ 10.
    a. Greater than0   b. Thing
    c. Undefined   d. Undefined

37. In common philosophical language, a proposition or _____, is the content of an assertion, that is, it is true-or-false and defined by the meaning of a particular piece of language.
    a. Statement0   b. Concept
    c. Undefined   d. Undefined

38. _____ are objects, characters, or other concrete representations of ideas, concepts, or other abstractions.
    a. Thing   b. Symbols0
    c. Undefined   d. Undefined

39. In mathematics, a _____ is a number which can be expressed as a ratio of two integers. Non-integer rational numbers (commonly called fractions) are usually written as the vulgar fraction a / b, where b is not zero.

Chapter 1. REAL NUMBERS AND ALGEBRAIC EXPRESSIONS

    a. Concept
    c. Undefined
    b. Rational Number0
    d. Undefined

40. In mathematics, an _____ is any real number that is not a rational number ¡ª that is, it is a number which cannot be expressed as m/n, where m and n are integers.
    a. Thing
    c. Undefined
    b. Irrational number0
    d. Undefined

41. In mathematics, _____ are any real number that is not a rational number ¡ª that is, it is a number which cannot be expressed as m/n, where m and n are integers.
    a. Irrational numbers0
    c. Undefined
    b. Thing
    d. Undefined

42. In plane geometry, a _____ is a polygon with four equal sides, four right angles, and parallel opposite sides. In algebra, the _____ of a number is that number multiplied by itself.
    a. Thing
    c. Undefined
    b. Square0
    d. Undefined

43. In mathematics, a _____ of a number x is a number r such that $r^2 = x$, or in words, a number r whose square (the result of multiplying the number by itself) is x.
    a. Square root0
    c. Undefined
    b. Thing
    d. Undefined

44. A _____ is a deliberate process for transforming one or more inputs into one or more results.
    a. Thing
    c. Undefined
    b. Calculation0
    d. Undefined

45. A _____ is a set whose members are members of another set or a set contained within another set.
    a. Thing
    c. Undefined
    b. Subset0
    d. Undefined

46. In mathematics, the _____ (or modulus) of a real number is its numerical value without regard to its sign.
    a. Thing
    c. Undefined
    b. Absolute value0
    d. Undefined

47. The _____ of measurement are a globally standardized and modernized form of the metric system.
    a. Units0
    c. Undefined
    b. Thing
    d. Undefined

48. In mathematics, the additive inverse, or _____ of a number n is the number that, when added to n, yields zero. The additive inverse of n is denoted −n. For example, 7 is −7, because 7 + (−7) = 0, and the additive inverse of −0.3 is 0.3, because −0.3 + 0.3 = 0.
    a. Thing
    c. Undefined
    b. Opposite0
    d. Undefined

Chapter 1. REAL NUMBERS AND ALGEBRAIC EXPRESSIONS

49. In mathematics, the _____ of a number n is the number that, when added to n, yields zero. The _____ of n is denoted −n. For example, 7 is −7, because 7 + (−7) = 0, and the _____ of −0.3 is 0.3, because −0.3 + 0.3 = 0.
   a. Additive inverse0
   b. Thing
   c. Undefined
   d. Undefined

50. In Euclidean geometry, a uniform _____ is a linear transformation that enlargers or diminishes objects, and whose _____ factor is the same in all directions. This is also called homothethy.
   a. Thing
   b. Scale0
   c. Undefined
   d. Undefined

51. In finance and economics, _____ is the process of finding the present value of an amount of cash at some future date, and along with compounding cash forms the basis of time value of money calculations.
   a. Discount0
   b. Thing
   c. Undefined
   d. Undefined

52. _____, in law and economics, is a form of risk management primarily used to hedge against the risk of a contingent loss.
   a. Thing
   b. Insurance0
   c. Undefined
   d. Undefined

53. In computing, a _____ can be defined as a structured collection of records or data that is stored in a computer so that a program can consult it to answer queries.
   a. Database0
   b. Thing
   c. Undefined
   d. Undefined

54. A _____ is a unit of length, usually used to measure distance, in a number of different systems, including Imperial units, United States customary units and Norwegian/Swedish mil. Its size can vary from system to system, but in each is between 1 and 10 kilometers. In contemporary English contexts _____ refers to either:
   a. Mile0
   b. Thing
   c. Undefined
   d. Undefined

55. _____ is a set, with some particular properties and usually some additional structure, such as the operations of addition or multiplication, for instance.
   a. Space0
   b. Thing
   c. Undefined
   d. Undefined

56. A _____ is a function that assigns a number to subsets of a given set.
   a. Measure0
   b. Thing
   c. Undefined
   d. Undefined

57. _____ is a unit of speed, expressing the number of international miles covered per hour.
   a. Thing
   b. Miles per hour0
   c. Undefined
   d. Undefined

58. In mathematics, a _____ is the end result of a division problem. It can also be expressed as the number of times the divisor divides into the dividend.

Chapter 1. REAL NUMBERS AND ALGEBRAIC EXPRESSIONS

a. Quotient0
b. Thing
c. Undefined
d. Undefined

59. A _____ is the result of the addition of a set of numbers. The numbers may be natural numbers, complex numbers, matrices, or still more complicated objects. An infinite _____ is a subtle procedure known as a series.
a. Thing
b. Sum0
c. Undefined
d. Undefined

60. The population _____ is the total number of human beings alive on the planet Earth at a given time.
a. Of the world0
b. Thing
c. Undefined
d. Undefined

61. The _____ (symbol _____) and the millibar (symbol mbar, also mb) are units of pressure.
a. Thing
b. Bar0
c. Undefined
d. Undefined

62. _____ is a mathematical operation, written a^n, involving two numbers, the base a and the exponent n.
a. Exponentiating0
b. Thing
c. Undefined
d. Undefined

63. _____ is a mathematical operation, written a^n, involving two numbers, the base a and the exponent n.
a. Thing
b. Exponentiation0
c. Undefined
d. Undefined

64. In mathematics, a _____ is the result of multiplying, or an expression that identifies factors to be multiplied.
a. Product0
b. Thing
c. Undefined
d. Undefined

65. In mathematics, factorization (British English: factorisation) or factoring is the decomposition of an object (for example, a number, a polynomial, or a matrix) into a product of other objects, or _____, which when multiplied together give the original.
a. Factors0
b. Thing
c. Undefined
d. Undefined

66. In mathematics, defined and _____ are used to explain whether or not expressions have meaningful, sensible, and unambiguous values.
a. Undefined0
b. Thing
c. Undefined
d. Undefined

67. _____, either of the curved-bracket punctuation marks that together make a set of _____
a. Thing
b. Parentheses0
c. Undefined
d. Undefined

68. A _____ is a three-dimensional solid object bounded by six square faces, facets, or sides, with three meeting at each vertex.

a. Cube0
b. Thing
c. Undefined
d. Undefined

69. A _____ of a number is a number a such that $a^3 = x$.
    a. Thing
    b. Cube root0
    c. Undefined
    d. Undefined

70. In abstract algebra, _____ consists of sets with binary operations that satisfy certain axioms.
    a. Thing
    b. Grouping0
    c. Undefined
    d. Undefined

71. A _____ is a numeral used to indicate a count. The most common use of the word today is to name the part of a fraction that tells the number or count of equal parts.
    a. Numerator0
    b. Thing
    c. Undefined
    d. Undefined

72. A _____ is the part of a fraction that tells how many equal parts make up a whole, and which is used in the name of the fraction: "halves", "thirds", "fourths" or "quarters", "fifths" and so on.
    a. Denominator0
    b. Concept
    c. Undefined
    d. Undefined

73. _____ is the transport of people on a trip/journey or the process or time involved in a person or object moving from one location to another.
    a. Thing
    b. Travel0
    c. Undefined
    d. Undefined

74. _____ is the fee paid on borrowed money.
    a. Interest0
    b. Thing
    c. Undefined
    d. Undefined

75. In Euclidean geometry, a _____ is the set of all points in a plane at a fixed distance, called the radius, from a given point, the center.
    a. Thing
    b. Circle0
    c. Undefined
    d. Undefined

76. In classical geometry, a _____ of a circle or sphere is any line segment from its center to its boundary. By extension, the _____ of a circle or sphere is the length of any such segment. The _____ is half the diameter. In science and engineering the term _____ of curvature is commonly used as a synonym for _____.
    a. Thing
    b. Radius0
    c. Undefined
    d. Undefined

77. Equivalence is the condition of being _____ or essentially equal.
    a. Thing
    b. Equivalent0
    c. Undefined
    d. Undefined

Chapter 1. REAL NUMBERS AND ALGEBRAIC EXPRESSIONS

78. _____ is a temperature scale named after the German physicist Daniel Gabriel _____ , who proposed it in 1724.
    a. Fahrenheit0
    b. Thing
    c. Undefined
    d. Undefined

79. _____ is, or relates to, the _____ temperature scale .
    a. Thing
    b. Celsius0
    c. Undefined
    d. Undefined

80. In mathematics, there are several meanings of _____ depending on the subject.
    a. Thing
    b. Degree0
    c. Undefined
    d. Undefined

81. _____ is a physical property of a system that underlies the common notions of hot and cold; something that is hotter has the greater _____.
    a. Temperature0
    b. Thing
    c. Undefined
    d. Undefined

82. The metre (or _____, see spelling differences) is a measure of length. It is the basic unit of length in the metric system and in the International System of Units (SI), used around the world for general and scientific purposes.
    a. Concept
    b. Meter0
    c. Undefined
    d. Undefined

83. The _____ of a geographic location is its height above a fixed reference point, often the mean sea level.
    a. Elevation0
    b. Thing
    c. Undefined
    d. Undefined

84. A _____ in statistics refers to a game in which the expected value is zero.
    a. Fair game0
    b. Thing
    c. Undefined
    d. Undefined

85. _____ or investing is a term with several closely-related meanings in business management, finance and economics, related to saving or deferring consumption.
    a. Investment0
    b. Thing
    c. Undefined
    d. Undefined

86. In mathematics, an _____, mean, or central tendency of a data set refers to a measure of the "middle" or "expected" value of the data set.
    a. Average0
    b. Concept
    c. Undefined
    d. Undefined

87. _____ is a way of expressing a number as a fraction of 100 per cent meaning "per hundred".
    a. Percent0
    b. Thing
    c. Undefined
    d. Undefined

88. Two mathematical objects are equal if and only if they are precisely the same in every way. This defines a binary relation, _____, denoted by the sign of _____ "=" in such a way that the statement "x = y" means that x and y are equal.
   a. Equality0
   b. Thing
   c. Undefined
   d. Undefined

89. In mathematics, the _____ inverse of a number x, denoted 1/x or x^{-1}, is the number which, when multiplied by x, yields 1. The _____ inverse of x is also called the reciprocal of x.
   a. Thing
   b. Multiplicative0
   c. Undefined
   d. Undefined

90. An _____ is an equality that remains true regardless of the values of any variables that appear within it, to distinguish it from an equality which is true under more particular conditions.
   a. Thing
   b. Identity0
   c. Undefined
   d. Undefined

91. In mathematics, the _____ inverse, or opposite, of a number n is the number that, when added to n, yields zero. The _____ inverse of n is denoted −n.
   a. Thing
   b. Additive0
   c. Undefined
   d. Undefined

92. In mathematics the _____ of a set which is equipped with the operation of addition is an element which, when added to any other element x in the set, yields x.
   a. Additive identity0
   b. Concept
   c. Undefined
   d. Undefined

93. In mathematics, the _____ of a number x, denoted 1/x or x^{-1}, is the number which, when multiplied by x, yields 1. The _____ of x is also called the reciprocal of x.
   a. Multiplicative inverse0
   b. Thing
   c. Undefined
   d. Undefined

94. _____ element of an element x with respect to a binary operation * with identity element e is an element y such that x * y = y * x = e. In particular,
   a. Thing
   b. Inverse0
   c. Undefined
   d. Undefined

95. The _____ is a property of multiplication or addition where the product or sum remains the same, regardless of whether or not the order of the addends or factors are changed.
   a. Commutative property0
   b. Thing
   c. Undefined
   d. Undefined

96. _____ is the act of putting ones into groups of 10.
   a. Regrouping0
   b. Thing
   c. Undefined
   d. Undefined

Chapter 1. REAL NUMBERS AND ALGEBRAIC EXPRESSIONS

97. In mathematics, _____ is a property that a binary operation can have. Within an expression containing two or more of the same associative operators in a row, the order of operations does not matter as long as the sequence of the operands is not changed.
    a. Thing
    b. Associativity0
    c. Undefined
    d. Undefined

98. In mathematics, and in particular in abstract algebra, the _____ is a property of binary operations that generalises the distributive law from elementary algebra.
    a. Distributive property0
    b. Thing
    c. Undefined
    d. Undefined

99. In Euclidean geometry, a _____ is moving every point a constant distance in a specified direction.
    a. Translation0
    b. Concept
    c. Undefined
    d. Undefined

100. In financial mathematics, the _____ volatility of an option contract is the volatility _____ by the market price of the option based on an option pricing model.
    a. Thing
    b. Implied0
    c. Undefined
    d. Undefined

101. In mathematics and logic, a _____ proof is a way of showing the truth or falsehood of a given statement by a straightforward combination of established facts, usually existing lemmas and theorems, without making any further assumptions.
    a. Thing
    b. Direct0
    c. Undefined
    d. Undefined

102. A pair of angles are _____ if the sum of their angles is 90°.
    a. Concept
    b. Complementary0
    c. Undefined
    d. Undefined

103. _____ means in succession or back-to-back
    a. Consecutive0
    b. Thing
    c. Undefined
    d. Undefined

104. An _____ is a number which is involved in addition. Numbers being added are considered to be the addends.
    a. Addend0
    b. Thing
    c. Undefined
    d. Undefined

105. In geometry, a _____ is defined as a quadrilateral where all four of its angles are right angles.
    a. Rectangle0
    b. Thing
    c. Undefined
    d. Undefined

106. _____ is a kind of property which exists as magnitude or multitude. It is among the basic classes of things along with quality, substance, change, and relation.

Chapter 1. REAL NUMBERS AND ALGEBRAIC EXPRESSIONS

    a. Thing
    b. Amount0
    c. Undefined
    d. Undefined

107. A pair of angles is _____ if their respective measures sum to 180 degrees.
    a. Supplementary0
    b. Concept
    c. Undefined
    d. Undefined

108. In set theory and other branches of mathematics, two kinds of complements are defined, the relative _____ and the absolute _____.
    a. Thing
    b. Complement0
    c. Undefined
    d. Undefined

109. In mathematics, a subset of Euclidean space R^n is called _____ if it is closed and bounded.
    a. Thing
    b. Compact0
    c. Undefined
    d. Undefined

110. The _____ of a solid object is the three-dimensional concept of how much space it occupies, often quantified numerically.
    a. Volume0
    b. Thing
    c. Undefined
    d. Undefined

111. In mathematics, a _____ is a quadric surface, with the following equation in Cartesian coordinates: $(x/_a)^2 + (y/_b)^2 = 1$.
    a. Cylinder0
    b. Thing
    c. Undefined
    d. Undefined

112. _____ is the distance around a given two-dimensional object. As a general rule, the _____ of a polygon can always be calculated by adding all the length of the sides together. So, the formula for triangles is P = a + b + c, where a, b and c stand for each side of it. For quadrilaterals the equation is P = a + b + c + d. For equilateral polygons, P = na, where n is the number of sides and a is the side length.
    a. Thing
    b. Perimeter0
    c. Undefined
    d. Undefined

113. An _____ is a straight line around which a geometric figure can be rotated.
    a. Thing
    b. Axis0
    c. Undefined
    d. Undefined

114. A bar chart, also known as a _____, is a chart with rectangular bars of lengths usually proportional to the magnitudes or frequencies of what they represent.
    a. Bar graph0
    b. Thing
    c. Undefined
    d. Undefined

115. In sociology and biology a _____ is the collection of people or organisms of a particular species living in a given geographic area or space, usually measured by a census.

a. Population0
b. Thing
c. Undefined
d. Undefined

116. The _____ integers are all the integers from zero on upwards.
    a. Thing
    b. Nonnegative0
    c. Undefined
    d. Undefined

117. _____ are procedures that allow people to exchange information by one of several methods.
    a. Communications0
    b. Thing
    c. Undefined
    d. Undefined

118. In probability theory, _____ are various sets of outcomes (a subset of the sample space) to which a probability is assigned.
    a. Thing
    b. Events0
    c. Undefined
    d. Undefined

119. _____ is a mathematical science pertaining to the collection, analysis, interpretation or explanation, and presentation of data. It is applicable to a wide variety of academic disciplines, from the physical and social sciences to the humanities.
    a. Statistics0
    b. Thing
    c. Undefined
    d. Undefined

120. _____ are economic entities that give rise to future economic benefit and is controlled by the entity as a result of past transaction or other events
    a. Thing
    b. Asset0
    c. Undefined
    d. Undefined

121. _____ is a synonym for information.
    a. Data0
    b. Thing
    c. Undefined
    d. Undefined

Chapter 2. EQUATIONS, INEQUALITIES, AND PROBLEM SOLVING

1. Transport or _____ is the movement of people and goods from one place to another.
    a. Transportation0
    b. Thing
    c. Undefined
    d. Undefined

2. _____ forms part of thinking. Considered the most complex of all intellectual functions, _____ has been defined as higher-order cognitive process that requires the modulation and control of more routine or fundamental skills.
    a. Problem solving0
    b. Thing
    c. Undefined
    d. Undefined

3. A _____ is a symbolic representation denoting a quantity or expression. It often represents an "unknown" quantity that has the potential to change.
    a. Variable0
    b. Thing
    c. Undefined
    d. Undefined

4. _____ is the design, analysis, and/or construction of works for practical purposes.
    a. Engineering0
    b. Thing
    c. Undefined
    d. Undefined

5. The word _____ comes from the Latin word linearis, which means created by lines.
    a. Linear0
    b. Thing
    c. Undefined
    d. Undefined

6. A _____ is an equation in which each term is either a constant or the product of a constant times the first power of a variable.
    a. Linear equation0
    b. Thing
    c. Undefined
    d. Undefined

7. In mathematics, an _____ is a statement about the relative size or order of two objects.
    a. Inequality0
    b. Thing
    c. Undefined
    d. Undefined

8. _____ interest refers to the fact that whenever interest is calculated, it is based not only on the original principal, but also on any unpaid interest that has been added to the principal.
    a. Thing
    b. Compound0
    c. Undefined
    d. Undefined

9. In mathematics, the _____ (or modulus) of a real number is its numerical value without regard to its sign.
    a. Absolute value0
    b. Thing
    c. Undefined
    d. Undefined

10. An _____ is an equality that remains true regardless of the values of any variables that appear within it, to distinguish it from an equality which is true under more particular conditions.
    a. Identity0
    b. Thing
    c. Undefined
    d. Undefined

11. In mathematics, _____ expressions is used to reduce the expression into the lowest possible term.

Chapter 2. EQUATIONS, INEQUALITIES, AND PROBLEM SOLVING

a. Simplifying0
b. Thing
c. Undefined
d. Undefined

12. In common philosophical language, a proposition or _____, is the content of an assertion, that is, it is true-or-false and defined by the meaning of a particular piece of language.
   a. Concept
   b. Statement0
   c. Undefined
   d. Undefined

13. An _____ is a combination of numbers, operators, grouping symbols and/or free variables and bound variables arranged in a meaningful way which can be evaluated..
   a. Thing
   b. Expression0
   c. Undefined
   d. Undefined

14. Two mathematical objects are equal if and only if they are precisely the same in every way. This defines a binary relation, _____, denoted by the sign of _____ "=" in such a way that the statement "x = y" means that x and y are equal.
   a. Thing
   b. Equality0
   c. Undefined
   d. Undefined

15. Equivalence is the condition of being _____ or essentially equal.
   a. Thing
   b. Equivalent0
   c. Undefined
   d. Undefined

16. In mathematics, a _____ may be described informally as a number that can be given by an infinite decimal representation.
   a. Thing
   b. Real number0
   c. Undefined
   d. Undefined

17. A _____ is a set of possible values that a variable can take on in order to satisfy a given set of conditions, which may include equations and inequalities.
   a. Solution set0
   b. Thing
   c. Undefined
   d. Undefined

18. In mathematics, _____ is an elementary arithmetic operation. When one of the numbers is a whole number, _____ is the repeated sum of the other number.
   a. Multiplication0
   b. Thing
   c. Undefined
   d. Undefined

19. A _____ is a negotiable instrument instructing a financial institution to pay a specific amount of a specific currency from a specific demand account held in the maker/depositor's name with that institution. Both the maker and payee may be natural persons or legal entities.
   a. Check0
   b. Thing
   c. Undefined
   d. Undefined

20. In abstract algebra, _____ consists of sets with binary operations that satisfy certain axioms.

Chapter 2. EQUATIONS, INEQUALITIES, AND PROBLEM SOLVING

   a. Grouping0
   c. Undefined
   b. Thing
   d. Undefined

21. _____ are objects, characters, or other concrete representations of ideas, concepts, or other abstractions.
   a. Symbols0
   c. Undefined
   b. Thing
   d. Undefined

22. _____, either of the curved-bracket punctuation marks that together make a set of _____
   a. Thing
   c. Undefined
   b. Parentheses0
   d. Undefined

23. In mathematics, and in particular in abstract algebra, the _____ is a property of binary operations that generalises the distributive law from elementary algebra.
   a. Distributive property0
   c. Undefined
   b. Thing
   d. Undefined

24. A _____ is the part of a fraction that tells how many equal parts make up a whole, and which is used in the name of the fraction: "halves", "thirds", "fourths" or "quarters", "fifths" and so on.
   a. Denominator0
   c. Undefined
   b. Concept
   d. Undefined

25. The decimal separator is a symbol used to mark the boundary between the integral and the fractional parts of a decimal numeral. Terms implying the symbol used are _____ and decimal comma.
   a. Decimal point0
   c. Undefined
   b. Concept
   d. Undefined

26. The material _____, also known as the material implication or truth functional _____, expresses a property of certain conditionals in logic.
   a. Conditional0
   c. Undefined
   b. Thing
   d. Undefined

27. In a mathematical proof or a syllogism, a _____ is a statement that is the logical consequence of preceding statements.
   a. Conclusion0
   c. Undefined
   b. Concept
   d. Undefined

28. _____ is the practice of doing mathematical calculations using only the human brain, with no help from any computing devices.
   a. Mental math0
   c. Undefined
   b. Concept
   d. Undefined

29. A _____ is the result of the addition of a set of numbers. The numbers may be natural numbers, complex numbers, matrices, or still more complicated objects. An infinite _____ is a subtle procedure known as a series.
   a. Thing
   c. Undefined
   b. Sum0
   d. Undefined

Chapter 2. EQUATIONS, INEQUALITIES, AND PROBLEM SOLVING

30. The _____ are the only integral domain whose positive elements are well-ordered, and in which order is preserved by addition. Like the natural numbers, the _____ form a countably infinite set. The set of all _____ is usually denoted in mathematics by a boldface Z.
    a. Thing
    b. Integers0
    c. Undefined
    d. Undefined

31. _____ means in succession or back-to-back
    a. Consecutive0
    b. Thing
    c. Undefined
    d. Undefined

32. A _____ is one of the basic shapes of geometry: a polygon with three vertices and three sides which are straight line segments.
    a. Triangle0
    b. Thing
    c. Undefined
    d. Undefined

33. _____ is the distance around a given two-dimensional object. As a general rule, the _____ of a polygon can always be calculated by adding all the length of the sides together. So, the formula for triangles is P = a + b + c, where a, b and c stand for each side of it. For quadrilaterals the equation is P = a + b + c + d. For equilateral polygons, P = na, where n is the number of sides and a is the side length.
    a. Perimeter0
    b. Thing
    c. Undefined
    d. Undefined

34. _____ is a branch of mathematics concerning the study of structure, relation and quantity.
    a. Concept
    b. Algebra0
    c. Undefined
    d. Undefined

35. A _____ is a special kind of ratio, indicating a relationship between two measurements with different units, such as miles to gallons or cents to pounds.
    a. Thing
    b. Rate0
    c. Undefined
    d. Undefined

36. _____ is a mathematical science pertaining to the collection, analysis, interpretation or explanation, and presentation of data. It is applicable to a wide variety of academic disciplines, from the physical and social sciences to the humanities.
    a. Thing
    b. Statistics0
    c. Undefined
    d. Undefined

37. _____ is a way of expressing a number as a fraction of 100 per cent meaning "per hundred".
    a. Thing
    b. Percent0
    c. Undefined
    d. Undefined

38. The _____, the average in everyday English, which is also called the arithmetic _____ (and is distinguished from the geometric _____ or harmonic _____). The average is also called the sample _____. The expected value of a random variable, which is also called the population _____.

Chapter 2. EQUATIONS, INEQUALITIES, AND PROBLEM SOLVING

   a. Thing
   b. Mean0
   c. Undefined
   d. Undefined

39. In mathematics, a _____ is the result of multiplying, or an expression that identifies factors to be multiplied.
   a. Product0
   b. Thing
   c. Undefined
   d. Undefined

40. _____ is a kind of property which exists as magnitude or multitude. It is among the basic classes of things along with quality, substance, change, and relation.
   a. Thing
   b. Amount0
   c. Undefined
   d. Undefined

41. The plus and _____ signs are mathematical symbols used to represent the notions of positive and negative as well as the operations of addition and subtraction.
   a. Thing
   b. Minus0
   c. Undefined
   d. Undefined

42. An _____ triange is a triangle with at least two sides of equal length.
   a. Thing
   b. Isosceles0
   c. Undefined
   d. Undefined

43. _____, from Latin meaning "to make progress", is defined in two different ways. Pure economic _____ is the increase in wealth that an investor has from making an investment, taking into consideration all costs associated with that investment including the opportunity cost of capital.
   a. Profit0
   b. Thing
   c. Undefined
   d. Undefined

44. _____ is the application of tools and a processing medium to the transformation of raw materials into finished goods for sale.
   a. Manufacturing0
   b. Thing
   c. Undefined
   d. Undefined

45. In plane geometry, a _____ is a polygon with four equal sides, four right angles, and parallel opposite sides. In algebra, the _____ of a number is that number multiplied by itself.
   a. Thing
   b. Square0
   c. Undefined
   d. Undefined

46. In geometry, a _____ is defined as a quadrilateral where all four of its angles are right angles.
   a. Rectangle0
   b. Thing
   c. Undefined
   d. Undefined

47. In set theory and other branches of mathematics, the _____ of a collection of sets is the set that contains everything that belongs to any of the sets, but nothing else.
   a. Thing
   b. Union0
   c. Undefined
   d. Undefined

Chapter 2. EQUATIONS, INEQUALITIES, AND PROBLEM SOLVING

48. In Euclidean geometry, a _____ is the set of all points in a plane at a fixed distance, called the radius, from a given point, the center.
    a. Circle0
    b. Thing
    c. Undefined
    d. Undefined

49. A _____ is a type of debt. All material things can be lent but this article focuses exclusively on monetary loans. Like all debt instruments, a _____ entails the redistribution of financial assets over time, between the lender and the borrower.
    a. Loan0
    b. Thing
    c. Undefined
    d. Undefined

50. _____ is a form of periodic payment from an employer to an employee, which is specified in an employment contract.
    a. Gross pay0
    b. Thing
    c. Undefined
    d. Undefined

51. A _____ is a form of periodic payment from an employer to an employee, which is specified in an employment contract.
    a. Salary0
    b. Thing
    c. Undefined
    d. Undefined

52. _____ is a synonym for information.
    a. Thing
    b. Data0
    c. Undefined
    d. Undefined

53. A _____ is a system of payment named after the small plastic card issued to users of the system.
    a. Thing
    b. Credit card0
    c. Undefined
    d. Undefined

54. _____, in economics and political economy, are the distributions or payments awarded to the various suppliers of the factors of production.
    a. Returns0
    b. Thing
    c. Undefined
    d. Undefined

55. In geometry, an _____ polygon is a polygon which has all sides of the same length.
    a. Thing
    b. Equilateral0
    c. Undefined
    d. Undefined

56. An _____ is a triangle in which all sides are of equal length.
    a. Equilateral triangle0
    b. Thing
    c. Undefined
    d. Undefined

57. In mathematics, an inequality is a statement about the relative size or order of two objects. For example 14 > 10, or 14 is _____ 10.

Chapter 2. EQUATIONS, INEQUALITIES, AND PROBLEM SOLVING

a. Greater than0
b. Thing
c. Undefined
d. Undefined

58. _____ is a set, with some particular properties and usually some additional structure, such as the operations of addition or multiplication, for instance.
   a. Thing
   b. Space0
   c. Undefined
   d. Undefined

59. _____ are a measure of time.
   a. Thing
   b. Minutes0
   c. Undefined
   d. Undefined

60. The metre (or _____, see spelling differences) is a measure of length. It is the basic unit of length in the metric system and in the International System of Units (SI), used around the world for general and scientific purposes.
   a. Meter0
   b. Concept
   c. Undefined
   d. Undefined

61. In mathematics, an _____, mean, or central tendency of a data set refers to a measure of the "middle" or "expected" value of the data set.
   a. Concept
   b. Average0
   c. Undefined
   d. Undefined

62. A _____ is a function that assigns a number to subsets of a given set.
   a. Thing
   b. Measure0
   c. Undefined
   d. Undefined

63. In set theory and other branches of mathematics, two kinds of complements are defined, the relative _____ and the absolute _____.
   a. Complement0
   b. Thing
   c. Undefined
   d. Undefined

64. _____ is a business term for the amount of money that a company receives from its activities in a given period, mostly from sales of products and/or services to customers
   a. Thing
   b. Revenue0
   c. Undefined
   d. Undefined

65. In mathematical logic, a Gödel numbering (or Gödel _____) is a function that assigns to each symbol and well-formed formula of some formal language a unique natural number called its Gödel number.
   a. Thing
   b. Code0
   c. Undefined
   d. Undefined

66. According to the United Nations Statistics Division, _____ is the resale sale without transformation of new and used goods to retailers, to industrial, commercial, institutional or professional users, or to other wholesalers, or involves acting as an agent or broker in buying merchandise for, or selling merchandise, to such persons or companies.

Chapter 2. EQUATIONS, INEQUALITIES, AND PROBLEM SOLVING

    a. Wholesale0
    b. Thing
    c. Undefined
    d. Undefined

67. The _____ of a solid object is the three-dimensional concept of how much space it occupies, often quantified numerically.
    a. Volume0
    b. Thing
    c. Undefined
    d. Undefined

68. In mathematics, _____ geometry was the traditional name for the geometry of three-dimensional Euclidean space — for practical purposes the kind of space we live in.
    a. Solid0
    b. Thing
    c. Undefined
    d. Undefined

69. A _____ is a quadrilateral, which is defined as a shape with four sides, which has a pair of parallel sides.
    a. Thing
    b. Trapezoid0
    c. Undefined
    d. Undefined

70. _____ is the fee paid on borrowed money.
    a. Thing
    b. Interest0
    c. Undefined
    d. Undefined

71. _____ refers to the fact that whenever interest is calculated, it is based not only on the original principal, but also on any unpaid interest that has been added to the principal. The more frequently interest is compounded, the faster the balance grows.
    a. Compound interest0
    b. Concept
    c. Undefined
    d. Undefined

72. A _____ is a deliberate process for transforming one or more inputs into one or more results.
    a. Calculation0
    b. Thing
    c. Undefined
    d. Undefined

73. A _____ is a unit of length, usually used to measure distance, in a number of different systems, including Imperial units, United States customary units and Norwegian/Swedish mil. Its size can vary from system to system, but in each is between 1 and 10 kilometers. In contemporary English contexts _____ refers to either:
    a. Thing
    b. Mile0
    c. Undefined
    d. Undefined

74. A _____ is a quantity that denotes the proportional amount or magnitude of one quantity relative to another.
    a. Thing
    b. Ratio0
    c. Undefined
    d. Undefined

75. _____ is, or relates to, the _____ temperature scale .
    a. Thing
    b. Celsius0
    c. Undefined
    d. Undefined

76. In mathematics, there are several meanings of _____ depending on the subject.

Chapter 2. EQUATIONS, INEQUALITIES, AND PROBLEM SOLVING

a. Thing
b. Degree0
c. Undefined
d. Undefined

77. _____ is a physical property of a system that underlies the common notions of hot and cold; something that is hotter has the greater _____.
a. Temperature0
b. Thing
c. Undefined
d. Undefined

78. _____ is a temperature scale named after the German physicist Daniel Gabriel _____, who proposed it in 1724.
a. Thing
b. Fahrenheit0
c. Undefined
d. Undefined

79. _____ is an expression of the effective interest rate that will be paid on a loan, taking into account one-time fees and standardizing the way the rate is expressed.
a. Annual percentage rate0
b. Thing
c. Undefined
d. Undefined

80. In mathematics, a _____ is a quadric surface, with the following equation in Cartesian coordinates: $(x/a)^2 + (y/b)^2 = 1$.
a. Thing
b. Cylinder0
c. Undefined
d. Undefined

81. _____ are activities that are governed by a set of rules or customs and often engaged in competitively.
a. Thing
b. Sports0
c. Undefined
d. Undefined

82. _____ is a unit of speed, expressing the number of international miles covered per hour.
a. Miles per hour0
b. Thing
c. Undefined
d. Undefined

83. The _____ is an imaginary line on the Earth's surface equidistant from the North Pole and South Pole.
a. Equator0
b. Thing
c. Undefined
d. Undefined

84. In physics, an _____ is the path that an object makes around another object while under the influence of a source of centripetal force, such as gravity.
a. Orbit0
b. Thing
c. Undefined
d. Undefined

85. The _____ is the distance around a closed curve. _____ is a kind of perimeter.
a. Thing
b. Circumference0
c. Undefined
d. Undefined

Chapter 2. EQUATIONS, INEQUALITIES, AND PROBLEM SOLVING

86. In classical geometry, a _____ of a circle or sphere is any line segment from its center to its boundary. By extension, the _____ of a circle or sphere is the length of any such segment. The _____ is half the diameter. In science and engineering the term _____ of curvature is commonly used as a synonym for _____.
   a. Radius0
   b. Thing
   c. Undefined
   d. Undefined

87. In sociology and biology a _____ is the collection of people or organisms of a particular species living in a given geographic area or space, usually measured by a census.
   a. Population0
   b. Thing
   c. Undefined
   d. Undefined

88. A _____ or CD is a time deposit, a financial product commonly offered to consumers by banks, thrift institutions, and credit unions.
   a. Certificate of deposit0
   b. Thing
   c. Undefined
   d. Undefined

89. U.S. liquid _____ is legally defined as 231 cubic inches, and is equal to 3.785411784 litres or abotu 0.13368 cubic feet. This is the most common definition of a _____. The U.S. fluid ounce is defined as 1/128 of a U.S. _____.
   a. Gallon0
   b. Thing
   c. Undefined
   d. Undefined

90. In mathematics, a _____ is the set of all points in three-dimensional space (R^3) which are at distance r from a fixed point of that space, where r is a positive real number called the radius of the _____. The fixed point is called the center or centre, and is not part of the _____ itself.
   a. Sphere0
   b. Thing
   c. Undefined
   d. Undefined

91. In geometry a _____, or deltoid, is a quadrilateral with two pairs of congruent adjacent sides.
   a. Thing
   b. Kite0
   c. Undefined
   d. Undefined

92. _____ is the transport of people on a trip/journey or the process or time involved in a person or object moving from one location to another.
   a. Travel0
   b. Thing
   c. Undefined
   d. Undefined

93. In geometry, a _____ (Greek words diairo = divide and metro = measure) of a circle is any straight line segment that passes through the centre and whose endpoints are on the circular boundary, or, in more modern usage, the length of such a line segment. When using the word in the more modern sense, one speaks of the _____ rather than a _____, because all diameters of a circle have the same length. This length is twice the radius. The _____ of a circle is also the longest chord that the circle has.
   a. Thing
   b. Diameter0
   c. Undefined
   d. Undefined

94. The _____ of measurement are a globally standardized and modernized form of the metric system.

Chapter 2. EQUATIONS, INEQUALITIES, AND PROBLEM SOLVING

a. Thing
b. Units0
c. Undefined
d. Undefined

95. A _____ is a unit of length in the metric system, equal to one thousand metres, the current SI base unit of length
   a. Kilometer0
   b. Thing
   c. Undefined
   d. Undefined

96. The _____ is a unit of length nearly equal to the semi-major axis of Earth's orbit around the Sun. The currently accepted value of the AU is 149 597 870 691 ± 30 metres.
   a. Thing
   b. Astronomical unit0
   c. Undefined
   d. Undefined

97. A _____, as defined by the International Astronomical Union, is a celestial body orbiting a star or stellar remnant that is massive enough to be rounded by its own gravity, not massive enough to cause thermonuclear fusion in its core, and has cleared its neighboring region of planetesimals.
   a. Planet0
   b. Thing
   c. Undefined
   d. Undefined

98. In mathematics, a class _____ is a structure used to organize the various Galois groups and modules that appear in class field theory. They were invented by Emil Artin and John Tate.
   a. Thing
   b. Formation0
   c. Undefined
   d. Undefined

99. _____ is the chance that something is likely to happen or be the case.
   a. Thing
   b. Probability0
   c. Undefined
   d. Undefined

100. If the probabilities of simple events are all the same, then they are _____. This occurs in a uniform sample space.
   a. Equally likely0
   b. Thing
   c. Undefined
   d. Undefined

101. Mathematical _____ is used to represent ideas.
   a. Thing
   b. Notation0
   c. Undefined
   d. Undefined

102. In elementary algebra, an _____ is a set that contains every real number between two indicated numbers and may contain the two numbers themselves.
   a. Thing
   b. Interval0
   c. Undefined
   d. Undefined

103. _____ is the notation in which permitted values for a variable are expressed as ranging over a certain interval; "5 < x < 9" is an example of the application of _____.
   a. Thing
   b. Interval notation0
   c. Undefined
   d. Undefined

Chapter 2. EQUATIONS, INEQUALITIES, AND PROBLEM SOLVING

104. A _____ is a one-dimensional picture in which the integers are shown as specially-marked points evenly spaced on a line.
 a. Thing
 b. Number line0
 c. Undefined
 d. Undefined

105. _____ is the state of being greater than any finite real or natural number, however large.
 a. Thing
 b. Infinite0
 c. Undefined
 d. Undefined

106. A _____ is a number that is less than zero.
 a. Thing
 b. Negative number0
 c. Undefined
 d. Undefined

107. In mathematics, _____ are essentially word problems that are designed to use mathematical critical thinking in everyday situations.
 a. Thing
 b. Application problems0
 c. Undefined
 d. Undefined

108. The payment of _____ as remuneration for services rendered or products sold is a common way to reward sales people.
 a. Commission0
 b. Thing
 c. Undefined
 d. Undefined

109. _____ is a mathematical notation for describing a set by stating the properties that its members must satisfy.
 a. Set-builder notation0
 b. Thing
 c. Undefined
 d. Undefined

110. Acid _____ ratio measures the ability of a company to use its near cash or quick assets to immediately extinguish its current liabilities.
 a. Thing
 b. Test0
 c. Undefined
 d. Undefined

111. In mathematics, a _____ is a two-dimensional manifold or surface that is perfectly flat.
 a. Plane0
 b. Thing
 c. Undefined
 d. Undefined

112. _____ usually refers to money in the form of liquid currency, such as banknotes or coins.
 a. Thing
 b. Cash0
 c. Undefined
 d. Undefined

113. The process of sending accounts to customers for goods or services is called _____.
 a. Billing0
 b. Thing
 c. Undefined
 d. Undefined

114. In mathematics, the _____ of two sets A and B is the set that contains all elements of A that also belong to B (or equivalently, all elements of B that also belong to A), but no other elements.

Chapter 2. EQUATIONS, INEQUALITIES, AND PROBLEM SOLVING

a. Intersection0
b. Thing
c. Undefined
d. Undefined

115. An _____ or member of a set is an object that when collected together make up the set.
    a. Thing
    b. Element0
    c. Undefined
    d. Undefined

116. In mathematics, the _____ , or members of a set or more generally a class are all those objects which when collected together make up the set or class.
    a. Elements0
    b. Thing
    c. Undefined
    d. Undefined

117. In mathematics, a subset of Euclidean space R^n is called _____ if it is closed and bounded.
    a. Thing
    b. Compact0
    c. Undefined
    d. Undefined

118. In mathematics, the _____ of a function is the set of all "output" values produced by that function. Given a function $f : A \to B$, the _____ of f, is defined to be the set $\{x \in B : x = f(a) \text{ for some } a \in A\}$.
    a. Thing
    b. Range0
    c. Undefined
    d. Undefined

119. The _____ is a temperature scale named after the German physicist Daniel Gabriel Fahrenheit (1686–1736), who proposed it in 1724.
    a. Fahrenheit scale0
    b. Thing
    c. Undefined
    d. Undefined

120. In Euclidean geometry, a uniform _____ is a linear transformation that enlargers or diminishes objects, and whose _____ factor is the same in all directions. This is also called homothethy.
    a. Scale0
    b. Thing
    c. Undefined
    d. Undefined

121. The _____ (symbol _____) and the millibar (symbol mbar, also mb) are units of pressure.
    a. Thing
    b. Bar0
    c. Undefined
    d. Undefined

122. In mathematics, the additive inverse, or _____ of a number n is the number that, when added to n, yields zero. The additive inverse of n is denoted −n. For example, 7 is −7, because 7 + (−7) = 0, and the additive inverse of −0.3 is 0.3, because −0.3 + 0.3 = 0.
    a. Opposite0
    b. Thing
    c. Undefined
    d. Undefined

123. In Graph theory, a _____ is a digraph with weighted edges.
    a. Network0
    b. Concept
    c. Undefined
    d. Undefined

Chapter 2. EQUATIONS, INEQUALITIES, AND PROBLEM SOLVING 27

124. In geometry, a line _____ is a part of a line that is bounded by two end points, and contains every point on the line between its end points.
 a. Concept
 b. Segment0
 c. Undefined
 d. Undefined

125. The _____ integers are all the integers from zero on upwards.
 a. Thing
 b. Nonnegative0
 c. Undefined
 d. Undefined

126. The State of _____ is a state located in the Rocky Mountain region of the United States of America.
 a. Thing
 b. Colorado0
 c. Undefined
 d. Undefined

127. Celsius is, or relates to, the Celsius temperature scale (previously known as the centigrade scale). The degree Celsius (symbol: °C) can refer to a specific temperature on the _____ as well as serve as unit increment to indicate a temperature interval (a difference between two temperatures or an uncertainty).
 a. Concept
 b. Celsius Scale0
 c. Undefined
 d. Undefined

128. In computing, a _____ can be defined as a structured collection of records or data that is stored in a computer so that a program can consult it to answer queries.
 a. Thing
 b. Database0
 c. Undefined
 d. Undefined

129. In economics, supply and _____ describe market relations between prospective sellers and buyers of a good.
 a. Demand0
 b. Thing
 c. Undefined
 d. Undefined

130. The _____ or kilogramme is the SI base unit of mass. It is defined as being equal to the mass of the international prototype of the _____.
 a. Thing
 b. Kilogram0
 c. Undefined
 d. Undefined

131. _____ is a term applied when talking about the movement of air from one place to the next.
 a. Thing
 b. Wind speed0
 c. Undefined
 d. Undefined

132. _____ has many meanings, most of which simply .
 a. Thing
 b. Power0
 c. Undefined
 d. Undefined

133. _____ is mass m per unit volume V.
 a. Thing
 b. Density0
 c. Undefined
 d. Undefined

Chapter 2. EQUATIONS, INEQUALITIES, AND PROBLEM SOLVING

134. In mathematics, a _____ can mean either an element of the set {1, 2, 3, ...} (i.e the positive integers) or an element of the set {0, 1, 2, 3, ...} (i.e. the non-negative integers).
 a. Concept
 b. Whole number0
 c. Undefined
 d. Undefined

135. In mathematics, a _____ can mean either an element of the set {1, 2, 3, ...} (i.e the positive integers or the counting numbers) or an element of the set {0, 1, 2, 3, ...} (i.e. the non-negative integers).
 a. Thing
 b. Natural number0
 c. Undefined
 d. Undefined

136. _____ is the interdisciplinary scientific study of the atmosphere that focuses on weather processes and forecasting.
 a. Thing
 b. Meteorology0
 c. Undefined
 d. Undefined

137. A _____ is a set of numbers that designate location in a given reference system, such as x,y in a planar _____ system or an x,y,z in a three-dimensional _____ system.
 a. Thing
 b. Coordinate0
 c. Undefined
 d. Undefined

138. _____ are the basic objects of study in graph theory. Informally speaking, a graph is a set of objects called points, nodes, or vertices connected by links called lines or edges.
 a. Thing
 b. Graphs0
 c. Undefined
 d. Undefined

139. A _____, is a symbolized depiction of space which highlights relations between components of that space. Most usually a _____ is a two-dimensional, geometrically accurate representation of a three-dimensional space.
 a. Map0
 b. Thing
 c. Undefined
 d. Undefined

Chapter 3. GRAPHS AND FUNCTIONS

1. A _____ is a symbolic representation denoting a quantity or expression. It often represents an "unknown" quantity that has the potential to change.
   a. Thing
   b. Variable0
   c. Undefined
   d. Undefined

2. _____ are the basic objects of study in graph theory. Informally speaking, a graph is a set of objects called points, nodes, or vertices connected by links called lines or edges.
   a. Graphs0
   b. Thing
   c. Undefined
   d. Undefined

3. _____ is often used to describe the measurement of the steepness, incline, gradient, or grade of a straight line. The _____ is defined as the ratio of the "rise" divided by the "run" between two points on a line, or in other words, the ratio of the altitude change to the horizontal distance between any two points on the line.
   a. Slope0
   b. Thing
   c. Undefined
   d. Undefined

4. In common philosophical language, a proposition or _____, is the content of an assertion, that is, it is true-or-false and defined by the meaning of a particular piece of language.
   a. Concept
   b. Statement0
   c. Undefined
   d. Undefined

5. The word _____ comes from the Latin word linearis, which means created by lines.
   a. Thing
   b. Linear0
   c. Undefined
   d. Undefined

6. A _____ is an equation in which each term is either a constant or the product of a constant times the first power of a variable.
   a. Thing
   b. Linear equation0
   c. Undefined
   d. Undefined

7. A _____ is a first degree polynomial mathematical function of the form: $f(x) = mx + b$ where m and b are real constants and x is a real variable.
   a. Linear function0
   b. Thing
   c. Undefined
   d. Undefined

8. In mathematics, an _____ is a statement about the relative size or order of two objects.
   a. Inequality0
   b. Thing
   c. Undefined
   d. Undefined

9. The mathematical concept of a _____ expresses the intuitive idea of deterministic dependence between two quantities, one of which is viewed as primary and the other as secondary. A _____ then is a way to associate a unique output for each input of a specified type, for example, a real number or an element of a given set.
   a. Thing
   b. Function0
   c. Undefined
   d. Undefined

10. An _____ is a collection of two not necessarily distinct objects, one of which is distinguished as the first coordinate and the other as the second coordinate.

Chapter 3. GRAPHS AND FUNCTIONS

a. Ordered pair0
b. Thing
c. Undefined
d. Undefined

11. In mathematics, the conjugate _____ or adjoint matrix of an m-by-n matrix A with complex entries is the n-by-m matrix A* obtained from A by taking the transpose and then taking the complex conjugate of each entry.
a. Thing
b. Pairs0
c. Undefined
d. Undefined

12. _____ is the estimation of a physical quantity such as distance, energy, temperature, or time.
a. Thing
b. Measurement0
c. Undefined
d. Undefined

13. _____ is a form of periodic payment from an employer to an employee, which is specified in an employment contract.
a. Gross pay0
b. Thing
c. Undefined
d. Undefined

14. A _____ is a form of periodic payment from an employer to an employee, which is specified in an employment contract.
a. Thing
b. Salary0
c. Undefined
d. Undefined

15. A _____ is a set of numbers that designate location in a given reference system, such as x,y in a planar _____ system or an x,y,z in a three-dimensional _____ system.
a. Coordinate0
b. Thing
c. Undefined
d. Undefined

16. In mathematics and its applications, a _____ is a system for assigning an n-tuple of numbers or scalars to each point in an n-dimensional space.
a. Coordinate system0
b. Concept
c. Undefined
d. Undefined

17. A _____ is a one-dimensional picture in which the integers are shown as specially-marked points evenly spaced on a line.
a. Thing
b. Number line0
c. Undefined
d. Undefined

18. An _____ is when two lines intersect somewhere on a plane creating a right angle at intersection
a. Axes0
b. Thing
c. Undefined
d. Undefined

19. An _____ is a straight line around which a geometric figure can be rotated.
a. Thing
b. Axis0
c. Undefined
d. Undefined

Chapter 3. GRAPHS AND FUNCTIONS

20. The _____ is the y- coordinate of a point within a two dimensional coordinate system. It is sometimes used to refer to the axis rather than the distance along the coordinate system.
   a. Thing
   b. Ordinate0
   c. Undefined
   d. Undefined

21. In mathematics, the _____ of a coordinate system is the point where the axes of the system intersect.
   a. Origin0
   b. Thing
   c. Undefined
   d. Undefined

22. In astronomy, geography, geometry and related sciences and contexts, a plane is said to be _____ at a given point if it is locally perpendicular to the gradient of the gravity field, i.e., with the direction of the gravitational force at that point.
   a. Horizontal0
   b. Thing
   c. Undefined
   d. Undefined

23. In mathematics, the _____ of two sets A and B is the set that contains all elements of A that also belong to B (or equivalently, all elements of B that also belong to A), but no other elements.
   a. Intersection0
   b. Thing
   c. Undefined
   d. Undefined

24. _____ consists of the first element in a coordinate pair. When graphed in the coordinate plane, it is the distance from the y-axis. Frequently called the x coordinate.
   a. Thing
   b. Abscissa0
   c. Undefined
   d. Undefined

25. In mathematics, a _____ is a two-dimensional manifold or surface that is perfectly flat.
   a. Plane0
   b. Thing
   c. Undefined
   d. Undefined

26. A _____ consists of one quarter of the coordinate plane.
   a. Quadrant0
   b. Thing
   c. Undefined
   d. Undefined

27. Mathematical _____ is used to represent ideas.
   a. Notation0
   b. Thing
   c. Undefined
   d. Undefined

28. _____ is the state of being greater than any finite real or natural number, however large.
   a. Thing
   b. Infinite0
   c. Undefined
   d. Undefined

29. In mathematics, a _____ is the result of multiplying, or an expression that identifies factors to be multiplied.
   a. Product0
   b. Thing
   c. Undefined
   d. Undefined

30. In mathematics, an inequality is a statement about the relative size or order of two objects. For example 14 > 10, or 14 is _____ 10.

Chapter 3. GRAPHS AND FUNCTIONS

    a. Thing
    b. Greater than0
    c. Undefined
    d. Undefined

31. _____ is a kind of property which exists as magnitude or multitude. It is among the basic classes of things along with quality, substance, change, and relation.
    a. Thing
    b. Amount0
    c. Undefined
    d. Undefined

32. The _____, the average in everyday English, which is also called the arithmetic _____ (and is distinguished from the geometric _____ or harmonic _____). The average is also called the sample _____. The expected value of a random variable, which is also called the population _____.
    a. Thing
    b. Mean0
    c. Undefined
    d. Undefined

33. A _____ of a number is the product of that number with any integer.
    a. Multiple0
    b. Thing
    c. Undefined
    d. Undefined

34. In mathematics, the concept of a _____ tries to capture the intuitive idea of a geometrical one-dimensional and continuous object. A simple example is the circle.
    a. Curve0
    b. Thing
    c. Undefined
    d. Undefined

35. In Euclidean geometry, a uniform _____ is a linear transformation that enlargers or diminishes objects, and whose _____ factor is the same in all directions. This is also called homothethy.
    a. Scale0
    b. Thing
    c. Undefined
    d. Undefined

36. In geometry, a _____ is defined as a quadrilateral where all four of its angles are right angles.
    a. Rectangle0
    b. Thing
    c. Undefined
    d. Undefined

37. _____ is the distance around a given two-dimensional object. As a general rule, the _____ of a polygon can always be calculated by adding all the length of the sides together. So, the formula for triangles is P = a + b + c, where a, b and c stand for each side of it. For quadrilaterals the equation is P = a + b + c + d. For equilateral polygons, P = na, where n is the number of sides and a is the side length.
    a. Thing
    b. Perimeter0
    c. Undefined
    d. Undefined

38. In mathematics and the mathematical sciences, a _____ is a fixed, but possibly unspecified, value. This is in contrast to a variable, which is not fixed.
    a. Constant0
    b. Thing
    c. Undefined
    d. Undefined

39. _____ is a term used in accounting, economics and finance with reference to the fact that assets with finite lives lose value over time.

Chapter 3. GRAPHS AND FUNCTIONS

a. Depreciation0
b. Thing
c. Undefined
d. Undefined

40. In plane geometry, a _____ is a polygon with four equal sides, four right angles, and parallel opposite sides. In algebra, the _____ of a number is that number multiplied by itself.
   a. Thing
   b. Square0
   c. Undefined
   d. Undefined

41. In mathematics, the _____ of a function is the set of all "output" values produced by that function. Given a function $f : A \to B$, the _____ of f, is defined to be the set $\{x \in B : x = f(a) \text{ for some } a \in A\}$.
   a. Range0
   b. Thing
   c. Undefined
   d. Undefined

42. In mathematics, a _____ of a k-place relation $L \subseteq X_1 \times \ldots \times X_k$ is one of the sets X_j, $1 \le j \le k$. In the special case where k = 2 and $L \subseteq X_1 \times X_2$ is a function $L : X_1 \to X_2$, it is conventional to refer to X_1 as the _____ of the function and to refer to X_2 as the codomain of the function.
   a. Thing
   b. Domain0
   c. Undefined
   d. Undefined

43. In mathematics, in the field of group theory, a _____ of a group is a quasisimple subnormal subgroup.
   a. Component0
   b. Concept
   c. Undefined
   d. Undefined

44. An _____ or member of a set is an object that when collected together make up the set.
   a. Element0
   b. Thing
   c. Undefined
   d. Undefined

45. The _____ are the only integral domain whose positive elements are well-ordered, and in which order is preserved by addition. Like the natural numbers, the _____ form a countably infinite set. The set of all _____ is usually denoted in mathematics by a boldface Z .
   a. Thing
   b. Integers0
   c. Undefined
   d. Undefined

46. _____ is a test to determine if a relation or its graph is a function or not
   a. Vertical line test0
   b. Thing
   c. Undefined
   d. Undefined

47. In mathematics, the _____ f is the collection of all ordered pairs . In particular, graph means the graphical representation of this collection, in the form of a curve or surface, together with axes, etc. Graphing on a Cartesian plane is sometimes referred to as curve sketching.
   a. Graph of a function0
   b. Thing
   c. Undefined
   d. Undefined

48. Acid _____ ratio measures the ability of a company to use its near cash or quick assets to immediately extinguish its current liabilities.

Chapter 3. GRAPHS AND FUNCTIONS

    a. Thing
    b. Test0
    c. Undefined
    d. Undefined

49. _____ is a synonym for information.
    a. Data0
    b. Thing
    c. Undefined
    d. Undefined

50. In mathematics, a _____ is a countable collection of open covers of a topological space that satisfies certain separation axioms.
    a. Thing
    b. Development0
    c. Undefined
    d. Undefined

51. The _____ of measurement are a globally standardized and modernized form of the metric system.
    a. Units0
    b. Thing
    c. Undefined
    d. Undefined

52. In Euclidean geometry, a _____ is the set of all points in a plane at a fixed distance, called the radius, from a given point, the center.
    a. Circle0
    b. Thing
    c. Undefined
    d. Undefined

53. In classical geometry, a _____ of a circle or sphere is any line segment from its center to its boundary. By extension, the _____ of a circle or sphere is the length of any such segment. The _____ is half the diameter. In science and engineering the term _____ of curvature is commonly used as a synonym for _____.
    a. Thing
    b. Radius0
    c. Undefined
    d. Undefined

54. The _____ of a solid object is the three-dimensional concept of how much space it occupies, often quantified numerically.
    a. Thing
    b. Volume0
    c. Undefined
    d. Undefined

55. A _____ is a three-dimensional solid object bounded by six square faces, facets, or sides, with three meeting at each vertex.
    a. Cube0
    b. Thing
    c. Undefined
    d. Undefined

56. A _____ is a function that assigns a number to subsets of a given set.
    a. Thing
    b. Measure0
    c. Undefined
    d. Undefined

57. A _____ fraction is a fraction in which the absolute value of the numerator is less than the denominator--hence, the absolute value of the fraction is less than 1.
    a. Thing
    b. Proper0
    c. Undefined
    d. Undefined

Chapter 3. GRAPHS AND FUNCTIONS

58. _____ is the production of food, feed, fiber, fuel and other goods by the systematic raizing of plants and animals.
   a. Thing
   b. Agriculture0
   c. Undefined
   d. Undefined

59. Any point where a graph makes contact with an coordinate axis is called an _____ of the graph
   a. Intercept0
   b. Thing
   c. Undefined
   d. Undefined

60. A _____ is a negotiable instrument instructing a financial institution to pay a specific amount of a specific currency from a specific demand account held in the maker/depositor's name with that institution. Both the maker and payee may be natural persons or legal entities.
   a. Check0
   b. Thing
   c. Undefined
   d. Undefined

61. In mathematics, a _____ may be described informally as a number that can be given by an infinite decimal representation.
   a. Thing
   b. Real number0
   c. Undefined
   d. Undefined

62. _____ is the application of tools and a processing medium to the transformation of raw materials into finished goods for sale.
   a. Manufacturing0
   b. Thing
   c. Undefined
   d. Undefined

63. A _____ is a unit of length, usually used to measure distance, in a number of different systems, including Imperial units, United States customary units and Norwegian/Swedish mil. Its size can vary from system to system, but in each is between 1 and 10 kilometers. In contemporary English contexts _____ refers to either:
   a. Thing
   b. Mile0
   c. Undefined
   d. Undefined

64. In geometry, the _____ of an object is a point in some sense in the middle of the object.
   a. Center0
   b. Thing
   c. Undefined
   d. Undefined

65. _____ is a mathematical science pertaining to the collection, analysis, interpretation or explanation, and presentation of data. It is applicable to a wide variety of academic disciplines, from the physical and social sciences to the humanities.
   a. Statistics0
   b. Thing
   c. Undefined
   d. Undefined

66. In geometry, two lines or planes if one falls on the other in such a way as to create congruent adjacent angles. The term may be used as a noun or adjective. Thus, referring to Figure 1, the line AB is the _____ to CD through the point B.
   a. Thing
   b. Perpendicular0
   c. Undefined
   d. Undefined

Chapter 3. GRAPHS AND FUNCTIONS

67. A _____ is a special kind of ratio, indicating a relationship between two measurements with different units, such as miles to gallons or cents to pounds.
   a. Thing
   b. Rate0
   c. Undefined
   d. Undefined

68. In mathematics, a _____ is a constant multiplicative factor of a certain object. The object can be such things as a variable, a vector, a function, etc. For example, the _____ of $9x^2$ is 9.
   a. Thing
   b. Coefficient0
   c. Undefined
   d. Undefined

69. In regression analysis, _____, also known as ordinary _____ analysis is a method for linear regression that determines the values of unknown quantities in a statistical model by minimizing the sum of the residuals difference between the predicted and observed values squared.
   a. Thing
   b. Least squares0
   c. Undefined
   d. Undefined

70. In mathematics, an _____, mean, or central tendency of a data set refers to a measure of the "middle" or "expected" value of the data set.
   a. Concept
   b. Average0
   c. Undefined
   d. Undefined

71. In mathematics, defined and _____ are used to explain whether or not expressions have meaningful, sensible, and unambiguous values.
   a. Undefined0
   b. Thing
   c. Undefined
   d. Undefined

72. The existence and properties of _____ are the basis of Euclid's parallel postulate. _____ are two lines on the same plane that do not intersect even assuming that lines extend to infinity in either direction.
   a. Thing
   b. Parallel lines0
   c. Undefined
   d. Undefined

73. In mathematics, the multiplicative inverse of a number x, denoted $1/x$ or x^{-1}, is the number which, when multiplied by x, yields 1. The multiplicative inverse of x is also called the _____ of x.
   a. Thing
   b. Reciprocal0
   c. Undefined
   d. Undefined

74. In linear algebra, the _____ of an n-by-n square matrix A is defined to be the sum of the elements on the main diagonal of A,
   a. Thing
   b. Trace0
   c. Undefined
   d. Undefined

75. In geographic information systems, a _____ comprises an entity with a geographic location, typically determined by points, arcs, or polygons. Carriageways and cadastres exemplify _____ data.
   a. Thing
   b. Feature0
   c. Undefined
   d. Undefined

Chapter 3. GRAPHS AND FUNCTIONS

76. A _____ is a landform that extends above the surrounding terrain in a limited area. A _____ is generally steeper than a hill, but there is no universally accepted standard definition for the height of a _____ or a hill although a _____ usually has an identifiable summit.
   a. Mountain0
   b. Thing
   c. Undefined
   d. Undefined

77. The _____ of a geographic location is its height above a fixed reference point, often the mean sea level.
   a. Thing
   b. Elevation0
   c. Undefined
   d. Undefined

78. In mathematics, there are several meanings of _____ depending on the subject.
   a. Degree0
   b. Thing
   c. Undefined
   d. Undefined

79. _____ is the level of functional and/or metabolic efficiency of an organism at both the micro level.
   a. Health0
   b. Thing
   c. Undefined
   d. Undefined

80. In mathematics, a _____ is any one of several different types of functions, mappings, operations, or transformations.
   a. Thing
   b. Projection0
   c. Undefined
   d. Undefined

81. _____ is the chance that something is likely to happen or be the case.
   a. Thing
   b. Probability0
   c. Undefined
   d. Undefined

82. A _____ is a numeral used to indicate a count. The most common use of the word today is to name the part of a fraction that tells the number or count of equal parts.
   a. Numerator0
   b. Thing
   c. Undefined
   d. Undefined

83. A _____ is the part of a fraction that tells how many equal parts make up a whole, and which is used in the name of the fraction: "halves", "thirds", "fourths" or "quarters", "fifths" and so on.
   a. Denominator0
   b. Concept
   c. Undefined
   d. Undefined

84. In mathematics, and in particular in abstract algebra, the _____ is a property of binary operations that generalises the distributive law from elementary algebra.
   a. Distributive property0
   b. Thing
   c. Undefined
   d. Undefined

85. In _____ algebra, a *-ring is an associative ring with an antilinear, antiautomorphism * : A ¨ A which is an involution.

Chapter 3. GRAPHS AND FUNCTIONS

    a. Star0   b. Thing
    c. Undefined   d. Undefined

86. _____ is a notation for writing numbers that is often used by scientists and mathematicians to make it easier to write large and small numbers.
    a. Scientific notation0   b. Thing
    c. Undefined   d. Undefined

87. In physics, _____ is an influence that may cause an object to accelerate. It may be experienced as a lift, a push, or a pull. The actual acceleration of the body is determined by the vector sum of all forces acting on it, known as net _____ or resultant _____.
    a. Force0   b. Thing
    c. Undefined   d. Undefined

88. In geometry, the relations of _____ are those such as 'lies on' between points and lines (as in 'point P lies on line L'), and 'intersects' (as in 'line L_1 intersects line L_2', in three-dimensional space). That is, they are the binary relations describing how subsets meet.
    a. Thing   b. Incidence0
    c. Undefined   d. Undefined

89. _____, from Latin meaning "to make progress", is defined in two different ways. Pure economic _____ is the increase in wealth that an investor has from making an investment, taking into consideration all costs associated with that investment including the opportunity cost of capital.
    a. Thing   b. Profit0
    c. Undefined   d. Undefined

90. In probability theory and statistics, a _____ is a number dividing the higher half of a sample, a population, or a probability distribution from the lower half.
    a. Concept   b. Median0
    c. Undefined   d. Undefined

91. In geometry, a line _____ is a part of a line that is bounded by two end points, and contains every point on the line between its end points.
    a. Concept   b. Segment0
    c. Undefined   d. Undefined

92. In geometry, an _____ is a point at which a line segment or ray terminates.
    a. Thing   b. Endpoint0
    c. Undefined   d. Undefined

93. A _____ is a part of a line that is bounded by two end points, and contains every point on the line between its end points.
    a. Thing   b. Line segment0
    c. Undefined   d. Undefined

94. _____ is the middle point of a line segment.

Chapter 3. GRAPHS AND FUNCTIONS

a. Midpoint0
b. Thing
c. Undefined
d. Undefined

95. In mathematics, _____ geometry was the traditional name for the geometry of three-dimensional Euclidean space — for practical purposes the kind of space we live in.
   a. Thing
   b. Solid0
   c. Undefined
   d. Undefined

96. In set theory and other branches of mathematics, the _____ of a collection of sets is the set that contains everything that belongs to any of the sets, but nothing else.
   a. Union0
   b. Thing
   c. Undefined
   d. Undefined

97. An _____ is a combination of numbers, operators, grouping symbols and/or free variables and bound variables arranged in a meaningful way which can be evaluated..
   a. Expression0
   b. Thing
   c. Undefined
   d. Undefined

98. _____ is a way of expressing a number as a fraction of 100 per cent meaning "per hundred".
   a. Percent0
   b. Thing
   c. Undefined
   d. Undefined

99. _____ is a regression method that models the relationship between a dependent variable Y, independent variables Xp, and a random term å.
   a. Linear regression0
   b. Thing
   c. Undefined
   d. Undefined

100. Two mathematical objects are equal if and only if they are precisely the same in every way. This defines a binary relation, _____, denoted by the sign of _____ "=" in such a way that the statement "x = y" means that x and y are equal.
   a. Thing
   b. Equality0
   c. Undefined
   d. Undefined

101. Equivalence is the condition of being _____ or essentially equal.
   a. Equivalent0
   b. Thing
   c. Undefined
   d. Undefined

102. _____ are procedures that allow people to exchange information by one of several methods.
   a. Thing
   b. Communications0
   c. Undefined
   d. Undefined

103. _____ systems represent systems whose behavior is not expressible as a sum of the behaviors of its descriptors.
   a. Thing
   b. Nonlinear0
   c. Undefined
   d. Undefined

Chapter 3. GRAPHS AND FUNCTIONS

104. In mathematics, the _____ inverse of a number x, denoted 1/x or x^{-1}, is the number which, when multiplied by x, yields 1. The _____ inverse of x is also called the reciprocal of x.
    a. Thing
    b. Multiplicative0
    c. Undefined
    d. Undefined

105. _____ element of an element x with respect to a binary operation * with identity element e is an element y such that x * y = y * x = e. In particular,
    a. Inverse0
    b. Thing
    c. Undefined
    d. Undefined

106. _____ is a branch of mathematics concerning the study of structure, relation and quantity.
    a. Concept
    b. Algebra0
    c. Undefined
    d. Undefined

107. A _____ is the result of the addition of a set of numbers. The numbers may be natural numbers, complex numbers, matrices, or still more complicated objects. An infinite _____ is a subtle procedure known as a series.
    a. Thing
    b. Sum0
    c. Undefined
    d. Undefined

108. _____ means in succession or back-to-back
    a. Thing
    b. Consecutive0
    c. Undefined
    d. Undefined

109. A _____ is a set of possible values that a variable can take on in order to satisfy a given set of conditions, which may include equations and inequalities.
    a. Solution set0
    b. Thing
    c. Undefined
    d. Undefined

110. Transport or _____ is the movement of people and goods from one place to another.
    a. Thing
    b. Transportation0
    c. Undefined
    d. Undefined

111. _____ is a set, with some particular properties and usually some additional structure, such as the operations of addition or multiplication, for instance.
    a. Thing
    b. Space0
    c. Undefined
    d. Undefined

112. A _____ signifies a point or points of probability on a subject e.g., the _____ of creativity, which allows for the formation of rule or norm or law by interpretation of the phenomena events that can be created.
    a. Thing
    b. Principle0
    c. Undefined
    d. Undefined

Chapter 4. SYSTEMS OF EQUATIONS

1. _____ are a set of equations containing multiple variables.
    a. Thing
    b. Systems of equations0
    c. Undefined
    d. Undefined

2. A _____ is an abstract model that uses mathematical language to describe the behavior of a system. Eykhoff defined a _____ as 'a representation of the essential aspects of an existing system which presents knowledge of that system in usable form'.
    a. Mathematical model0
    b. Thing
    c. Undefined
    d. Undefined

3. _____ is a business term for the amount of money that a company receives from its activities in a given period, mostly from sales of products and/or services to customers
    a. Revenue0
    b. Thing
    c. Undefined
    d. Undefined

4. The _____ of measurement are a globally standardized and modernized form of the metric system.
    a. Thing
    b. Units0
    c. Undefined
    d. Undefined

5. _____ is a kind of property which exists as magnitude or multitude. It is among the basic classes of things along with quality, substance, change, and relation.
    a. Amount0
    b. Thing
    c. Undefined
    d. Undefined

6. The _____, the average in everyday English, which is also called the arithmetic _____ (and is distinguished from the geometric _____ or harmonic _____). The average is also called the sample _____. The expected value of a random variable, which is also called the population _____.
    a. Thing
    b. Mean0
    c. Undefined
    d. Undefined

7. In mathematics, the _____ of two sets A and B is the set that contains all elements of A that also belong to B (or equivalently, all elements of B that also belong to A), but no other elements.
    a. Thing
    b. Intersection0
    c. Undefined
    d. Undefined

8. In mathematics, an inequality is a statement about the relative size or order of two objects. For example 14 > 10, or 14 is _____ 10.
    a. Greater than0
    b. Thing
    c. Undefined
    d. Undefined

9. _____ is the application of tools and a processing medium to the transformation of raw materials into finished goods for sale.
    a. Thing
    b. Manufacturing0
    c. Undefined
    d. Undefined

10. A _____ is a symbolic representation denoting a quantity or expression. It often represents an "unknown" quantity that has the potential to change.

Chapter 4. SYSTEMS OF EQUATIONS

    a. Thing
    c. Undefined
    b. Variable0
    d. Undefined

11. The word _____ comes from the Latin word linearis, which means created by lines.
    a. Thing
    b. Linear0
    c. Undefined
    d. Undefined

12. A _____ is an equation in which each term is either a constant or the product of a constant times the first power of a variable.
    a. Linear equation0
    b. Thing
    c. Undefined
    d. Undefined

13. An _____ is a collection of two not necessarily distinct objects, one of which is distinguished as the first coordinate and the other as the second coordinate.
    a. Thing
    b. Ordered pair0
    c. Undefined
    d. Undefined

14. In mathematics, a _____ is a two-dimensional manifold or surface that is perfectly flat.
    a. Thing
    b. Plane0
    c. Undefined
    d. Undefined

15. A _____ is a negotiable instrument instructing a financial institution to pay a specific amount of a specific currency from a specific demand account held in the maker/depositor's name with that institution. Both the maker and payee may be natural persons or legal entities.
    a. Thing
    b. Check0
    c. Undefined
    d. Undefined

16. A _____ is a set of numbers that designate location in a given reference system, such as x,y in a planar _____ system or an x,y,z in a three-dimensional _____ system.
    a. Thing
    b. Coordinate0
    c. Undefined
    d. Undefined

17. _____ are the basic objects of study in graph theory. Informally speaking, a graph is a set of objects called points, nodes, or vertices connected by links called lines or edges.
    a. Graphs0
    b. Thing
    c. Undefined
    d. Undefined

18. _____ is often used to describe the measurement of the steepness, incline, gradient, or grade of a straight line. The _____ is defined as the ratio of the "rise" divided by the "run" between two points on a line, or in other words, the ratio of the altitude change to the horizontal distance between any two points on the line.
    a. Slope0
    b. Thing
    c. Undefined
    d. Undefined

19. A _____ is a set of possible values that a variable can take on in order to satisfy a given set of conditions, which may include equations and inequalities.

Chapter 4. SYSTEMS OF EQUATIONS

    a. Solution set0
    b. Thing
    c. Undefined
    d. Undefined

20. In mathematics, the conjugate _____ or adjoint matrix of an m-by-n matrix A with complex entries is the n-by-m matrix A* obtained from A by taking the transpose and then taking the complex conjugate of each entry.
    a. Thing
    b. Pairs0
    c. Undefined
    d. Undefined

21. _____ is the state of being greater than any finite real or natural number, however large.
    a. Infinite0
    b. Thing
    c. Undefined
    d. Undefined

22. The _____ is used to discard one of the variables in an equation, only to replace it with the actual value when solving multiple equations.
    a. Substitution method0
    b. Thing
    c. Undefined
    d. Undefined

23. An _____ is a combination of numbers, operators, grouping symbols and/or free variables and bound variables arranged in a meaningful way which can be evaluated..
    a. Expression0
    b. Thing
    c. Undefined
    d. Undefined

24. In mathematics, a _____ is a constant multiplicative factor of a certain object. The object can be such things as a variable, a vector, a function, etc. For example, the _____ of $9x^2$ is 9.
    a. Thing
    b. Coefficient0
    c. Undefined
    d. Undefined

25. The Gaussian _____ is an algorithm which can be used to determine the solutions of a system of linear equations, to find the rank of a matrix, and to calculate the inverse of an invertible square matrix.
    a. Elimination method0
    b. Thing
    c. Undefined
    d. Undefined

26. In mathematics, the additive inverse, or _____ of a number n is the number that, when added to n, yields zero. The additive inverse of n is denoted −n. For example, 7 is −7, because 7 + (−7) = 0, and the additive inverse of −0.3 is 0.3, because −0.3 + 0.3 = 0.
    a. Opposite0
    b. Thing
    c. Undefined
    d. Undefined

27. _____ is a notation for writing numbers that is often used by scientists and mathematicians to make it easier to write large and small numbers.
    a. Scientific notation0
    b. Thing
    c. Undefined
    d. Undefined

28. In mathematics, the _____ of a number n is the number that, when added to n, yields zero. The _____ of n is denoted −n. For example, 7 is −7, because 7 + (−7) = 0, and the _____ of −0.3 is 0.3, because −0.3 + 0.3 = 0.

Chapter 4. SYSTEMS OF EQUATIONS

a. Additive inverse0
b. Thing
c. Undefined
d. Undefined

29. A _____ is the result of the addition of a set of numbers. The numbers may be natural numbers, complex numbers, matrices, or still more complicated objects. An infinite _____ is a subtle procedure known as a series.
    a. Sum0
    b. Thing
    c. Undefined
    d. Undefined

30. The existence and properties of _____ are the basis of Euclid's parallel postulate. _____ are two lines on the same plane that do not intersect even assuming that lines extend to infinity in either direction.
    a. Parallel lines0
    b. Thing
    c. Undefined
    d. Undefined

31. U.S. liquid _____ is legally defined as 231 cubic inches, and is equal to 3.785411784 litres or abotu 0.13368 cubic feet. This is the most common definition of a _____. The U.S. fluid ounce is defined as 1/128 of a U.S. _____.
    a. Thing
    b. Gallon0
    c. Undefined
    d. Undefined

32. In linear algebra, the _____ of an n-by-n square matrix A is defined to be the sum of the elements on the main diagonal of A,
    a. Thing
    b. Trace0
    c. Undefined
    d. Undefined

33. In geographic information systems, a _____ comprises an entity with a geographic location, typically determined by points, arcs, or polygons. Carriageways and cadastres exemplify _____ data.
    a. Thing
    b. Feature0
    c. Undefined
    d. Undefined

34. _____ is the practice of doing mathematical calculations using only the human brain, with no help from any computing devices.
    a. Mental math0
    b. Concept
    c. Undefined
    d. Undefined

35. In economics, supply and _____ describe market relations between prospective sellers and buyers of a good.
    a. Thing
    b. Demand0
    c. Undefined
    d. Undefined

36. In economics, economic _____ is simply a state of the world where economic forces are balanced and in the absence of external influences the values of economic variables will not change.
    a. Equilibrium0
    b. Thing
    c. Undefined
    d. Undefined

37. _____ is a synonym for information.

Chapter 4. SYSTEMS OF EQUATIONS

a. Data0
b. Thing
c. Undefined
d. Undefined

38. _____ is the production of food, feed, fiber, fuel and other goods by the systematic raizing of plants and animals.
    a. Agriculture0
    b. Thing
    c. Undefined
    d. Undefined

39. In mathematics, a _____ can mean either an element of the set {1, 2, 3, ...} (i.e the positive integers) or an element of the set {0, 1, 2, 3, ...} (i.e. the non-negative integers).
    a. Concept
    b. Whole number0
    c. Undefined
    d. Undefined

40. _____ is a mathematical science pertaining to the collection, analysis, interpretation or explanation, and presentation of data. It is applicable to a wide variety of academic disciplines, from the physical and social sciences to the humanities.
    a. Statistics0
    b. Thing
    c. Undefined
    d. Undefined

41. In mathematics, _____ are two-dimensional manifolds or surfaces that are perfectly flat.
    a. Thing
    b. Planes0
    c. Undefined
    d. Undefined

42. In geometry, _____ lines are two lines that share one or more common points.
    a. Thing
    b. Intersecting0
    c. Undefined
    d. Undefined

43. In common philosophical language, a proposition or _____, is the content of an assertion, that is, it is true-or-false and defined by the meaning of a particular piece of language.
    a. Concept
    b. Statement0
    c. Undefined
    d. Undefined

44. In mathematics and more specifically set theory, the _____ set is the unique set which contains no elements.
    a. Empty0
    b. Thing
    c. Undefined
    d. Undefined

45. A _____ is a special kind of ratio, indicating a relationship between two measurements with different units, such as miles to gallons or cents to pounds.
    a. Thing
    b. Rate0
    c. Undefined
    d. Undefined

46. _____ forms part of thinking. Considered the most complex of all intellectual functions, _____ has been defined as higher-order cognitive process that requires the modulation and control of more routine or fundamental skills.
    a. Problem solving0
    b. Thing
    c. Undefined
    d. Undefined

Chapter 4. SYSTEMS OF EQUATIONS

47. A _____ is a unit of length, usually used to measure distance, in a number of different systems, including Imperial units, United States customary units and Norwegian/Swedish mil. Its size can vary from system to system, but in each is between 1 and 10 kilometers. In contemporary English contexts _____ refers to either:
   a. Mile0   b. Thing
   c. Undefined   d. Undefined

48. _____ is the transport of people on a trip/journey or the process or time involved in a person or object moving from one location to another.
   a. Thing   b. Travel0
   c. Undefined   d. Undefined

49. A _____ is one of the basic shapes of geometry: a polygon with three vertices and three sides which are straight line segments.
   a. Triangle0   b. Thing
   c. Undefined   d. Undefined

50. A _____ is a function that assigns a number to subsets of a given set.
   a. Measure0   b. Thing
   c. Undefined   d. Undefined

51. In mathematics, there are several meanings of _____ depending on the subject.
   a. Degree0   b. Thing
   c. Undefined   d. Undefined

52. A _____ is a polygon with four sides and four vertices.
   a. Quadrilateral0   b. Thing
   c. Undefined   d. Undefined

53. _____ is the distance around a given two-dimensional object. As a general rule, the _____ of a polygon can always be calculated by adding all the length of the sides together. So, the formula for triangles is P = a + b + c, where a, b and c stand for each side of it. For quadrilaterals the equation is P = a + b + c + d. For equilateral polygons, P = na, where n is the number of sides and a is the side length.
   a. Thing   b. Perimeter0
   c. Undefined   d. Undefined

54. In geometry a _____ is a plane figure that is bounded by a closed path or circuit, composed of a finite number of sequential line segments.
   a. Polygon0   b. Thing
   c. Undefined   d. Undefined

55. The plus and _____ signs are mathematical symbols used to represent the notions of positive and negative as well as the operations of addition and subtraction.
   a. Thing   b. Minus0
   c. Undefined   d. Undefined

56. A _____ is a unit of length in the metric system, equal to one thousand metres, the current SI base unit of length

Chapter 4. SYSTEMS OF EQUATIONS

    a. Thing
    b. Kilometer0
    c. Undefined
    d. Undefined

57. _____ is a form of periodic payment from an employer to an employee, which is specified in an employment contract.
    a. Gross pay0
    b. Thing
    c. Undefined
    d. Undefined

58. The payment of _____ as remuneration for services rendered or products sold is a common way to reward sales people.
    a. Commission0
    b. Thing
    c. Undefined
    d. Undefined

59. A _____ is a form of periodic payment from an employer to an employee, which is specified in an employment contract.
    a. Salary0
    b. Thing
    c. Undefined
    d. Undefined

60. The mathematical concept of a _____ expresses the intuitive idea of deterministic dependence between two quantities, one of which is viewed as primary and the other as secondary. A _____ then is a way to associate a unique output for each input of a specified type, for example, a real number or an element of a given set.
    a. Thing
    b. Function0
    c. Undefined
    d. Undefined

61. In combinatorial mathematics, given a collection C of disjoint sets, a _____ is a set containing exactly one element from each member of the collection: it is a section of the quotient map induced by the collection.
    a. Thing
    b. Transversal0
    c. Undefined
    d. Undefined

62. _____ is the largest city in the state of Texas and the fourth-largest in the United States. As of the 2005 U.S. Census estimate, it had a population of more than 2 million.
    a. Houston0
    b. Thing
    c. Undefined
    d. Undefined

63. _____ is the chance that something is likely to happen or be the case.
    a. Probability0
    b. Thing
    c. Undefined
    d. Undefined

64. In geometry, the _____ of an object is a point in some sense in the middle of the object.
    a. Center0
    b. Thing
    c. Undefined
    d. Undefined

65. In mathematics, a _____ is a rectangular table of numbers or, more generally, a table consisting of abstract quantities that can be added and multiplied.

Chapter 4. SYSTEMS OF EQUATIONS

    a. Thing
    b. Matrix0
    c. Undefined
    d. Undefined

66. In mathematics, a matrix can be thought of as each row or _____ being a vector. Hence, a space formed by row vectors or _____ vectors are said to be a row space or a _____ space.
    a. Concept
    b. Column0
    c. Undefined
    d. Undefined

67. Equivalence is the condition of being _____ or essentially equal.
    a. Thing
    b. Equivalent0
    c. Undefined
    d. Undefined

68. An _____ or member of a set is an object that when collected together make up the set.
    a. Thing
    b. Element0
    c. Undefined
    d. Undefined

69. In mathematics, the _____ , or members of a set or more generally a class are all those objects which when collected together make up the set or class.
    a. Elements0
    b. Thing
    c. Undefined
    d. Undefined

70. A _____ can refer to a line joining two nonadjacent vertices of a polygon or polyhedron, or in some contexts any upward or downward sloping line. .
    a. Diagonal0
    b. Thing
    c. Undefined
    d. Undefined

71. _____ are elementary linear transformations on a matrix which preserve matrix equivalence.
    a. Elementary row operations0
    b. Thing
    c. Undefined
    d. Undefined

72. Elementary _____ are simple transformations which can be applied to a matrix without changing the linear system of equations that it represents.
    a. Row operations0
    b. Thing
    c. Undefined
    d. Undefined

73. Transport or _____ is the movement of people and goods from one place to another.
    a. Transportation0
    b. Thing
    c. Undefined
    d. Undefined

74. _____ is a way of expressing a number as a fraction of 100 per cent meaning "per hundred".
    a. Thing
    b. Percent0
    c. Undefined
    d. Undefined

75. In mathematics, the _____ f is the collection of all ordered pairs . In particular, graph means the graphical representation of this collection, in the form of a curve or surface, together with axes, etc. Graphing on a Cartesian plane is sometimes referred to as curve sketching.

Chapter 4. SYSTEMS OF EQUATIONS

a. Graph of a function0
b. Thing
c. Undefined
d. Undefined

76. In algebra, a _____ is a function depending on *n* that associates a scalar, det(A), to every *n×n* square matrix A.
    a. Thing
    b. Determinant0
    c. Undefined
    d. Undefined

77. In computer science an _____ is a data structure that consists of a group of elements having a single name that are accessed by indexing. In most programming languages each element has the same data type and the _____ occupies a continuous area of storage.
    a. Array0
    b. Thing
    c. Undefined
    d. Undefined

78. _____, verti-bar, vertical line, divider line, or pipe is the name of the character .
    a. Vertical bar0
    b. Thing
    c. Undefined
    d. Undefined

79. In plane geometry, a _____ is a polygon with four equal sides, four right angles, and parallel opposite sides. In algebra, the _____ of a number is that number multiplied by itself.
    a. Square0
    b. Thing
    c. Undefined
    d. Undefined

80. The _____ (symbol _____) and the millibar (symbol mbar, also mb) are units of pressure.
    a. Bar0
    b. Thing
    c. Undefined
    d. Undefined

81. Mathematical _____ is used to represent ideas.
    a. Thing
    b. Notation0
    c. Undefined
    d. Undefined

82. A _____ is a numeral used to indicate a count. The most common use of the word today is to name the part of a fraction that tells the number or count of equal parts.
    a. Thing
    b. Numerator0
    c. Undefined
    d. Undefined

83. A _____ is the part of a fraction that tells how many equal parts make up a whole, and which is used in the name of the fraction: "halves", "thirds", "fourths" or "quarters", "fifths" and so on.
    a. Denominator0
    b. Concept
    c. Undefined
    d. Undefined

84. In mathematics and the mathematical sciences, a _____ is a fixed, but possibly unspecified, value. This is in contrast to a variable, which is not fixed.
    a. Thing
    b. Constant0
    c. Undefined
    d. Undefined

85. In linear algebra, a _____ of a matrix A is the determinant of some smaller square matrix, cut down from A.

Chapter 4. SYSTEMS OF EQUATIONS

a. Minor0
b. Thing
c. Undefined
d. Undefined

86. In mathematics, a _____ is an n-tuple with n being 3.
a. Triple0
b. Thing
c. Undefined
d. Undefined

87. In mathematics, a _____ may be described informally as a number that can be given by an infinite decimal representation.
a. Real number0
b. Thing
c. Undefined
d. Undefined

88. _____ is the general term that is used to describe physical artifacts of a technology.
a. Thing
b. Hardware0
c. Undefined
d. Undefined

89. In chemistry, a _____ is substance made by combining two or more different materials in such a way that no chemical reaction occurs.
a. Thing
b. Mixture0
c. Undefined
d. Undefined

90. _____ is the fee paid on borrowed money.
a. Thing
b. Interest0
c. Undefined
d. Undefined

91. _____ or investing is a term with several closely-related meanings in business management, finance and economics, related to saving or deferring consumption.
a. Thing
b. Investment0
c. Undefined
d. Undefined

92. An _____ triange is a triangle with at least two sides of equal length.
a. Thing
b. Isosceles0
c. Undefined
d. Undefined

93. _____ element of an element x with respect to a binary operation * with identity element e is an element y such that x * y = y * x = e. In particular,
a. Inverse0
b. Thing
c. Undefined
d. Undefined

94. In mathematics, the _____ inverse, or opposite, of a number n is the number that, when added to n, yields zero. The _____ inverse of n is denoted −n.
a. Additive0
b. Thing
c. Undefined
d. Undefined

95. In mathematics, and in particular in abstract algebra, the _____ is a property of binary operations that generalises the distributive law from elementary algebra.

Chapter 4. SYSTEMS OF EQUATIONS

a. Thing
b. Distributive property0
c. Undefined
d. Undefined

96. _____, from Latin meaning "to make progress", is defined in two different ways. Pure economic _____ is the increase in wealth that an investor has from making an investment, taking into consideration all costs associated with that investment including the opportunity cost of capital.
a. Profit0
b. Thing
c. Undefined
d. Undefined

97. A _____ consists of one quarter of the coordinate plane.
a. Thing
b. Quadrant0
c. Undefined
d. Undefined

98. In mathematics and its applications, a _____ is a system for assigning an n-tuple of numbers or scalars to each point in an n-dimensional space.
a. Concept
b. Coordinate system0
c. Undefined
d. Undefined

99. _____ means of or relating to the French philosopher and mathematician Renê Descartes.
a. Thing
b. Cartesian0
c. Undefined
d. Undefined

100. In mathematics, the _____ is used to determine each point uniquely in a plane through two numbers, usually called the x-coordinate and the y-coordinate of the point.
a. Thing
b. Cartesian coordinate system0
c. Undefined
d. Undefined

101. A circular _____ or circle _____ also known as a pie piece is the portion of a circle enclosed by two radii and an arc.
a. Thing
b. Sector0
c. Undefined
d. Undefined

102. _____ is the estimation of a physical quantity such as distance, energy, temperature, or time.
a. Thing
b. Measurement0
c. Undefined
d. Undefined

Chapter 5. EXPONENTS, POLYNOMIALS, AND POLYNOMIAL FUNCTIONS

1. A _____ is a polynomial consisting of three terms; in other words, it is the sum of three monomials.
   a. Thing
   b. Trinomial0
   c. Undefined
   d. Undefined

2. _____ forms part of thinking. Considered the most complex of all intellectual functions, _____ has been defined as higher-order cognitive process that requires the modulation and control of more routine or fundamental skills.
   a. Thing
   b. Problem solving0
   c. Undefined
   d. Undefined

3. In mathematics, a _____ is the result of multiplying, or an expression that identifies factors to be multiplied.
   a. Product0
   b. Thing
   c. Undefined
   d. Undefined

4. In mathematics, the _____ divisor of two non-zero integers, is the largest positive integer that divides both numbers without remainder.
   a. Greatest common0
   b. Thing
   c. Undefined
   d. Undefined

5. In Math the greates common divisor sometimes known as the _____ of two non- zero integers.
   a. Thing
   b. Greatest common factor0
   c. Undefined
   d. Undefined

6. In abstract algebra, _____ consists of sets with binary operations that satisfy certain axioms.
   a. Grouping0
   b. Thing
   c. Undefined
   d. Undefined

7. Mathematical _____ is used to represent ideas.
   a. Notation0
   b. Thing
   c. Undefined
   d. Undefined

8. _____ is the largest positive integer that divides both numbers without remainder.
   a. Thing
   b. Common Factor0
   c. Undefined
   d. Undefined

9. _____ is a mathematical operation, written a^n, involving two numbers, the base a and the exponent n.
   a. Thing
   b. Exponentiating0
   c. Undefined
   d. Undefined

10. _____ is a mathematical operation, written a^n, involving two numbers, the base a and the exponent n.
    a. Thing
    b. Exponentiation0
    c. Undefined
    d. Undefined

11. In mathematics, _____ is the decomposition of an object into a product of other objects, or factors, which when multiplied together give the original.
    a. Thing
    b. Factoring0
    c. Undefined
    d. Undefined

Chapter 5. EXPONENTS, POLYNOMIALS, AND POLYNOMIAL FUNCTIONS

12. The word _____ comes from the Latin word linearis, which means created by lines.
   a. Linear0
   b. Thing
   c. Undefined
   d. Undefined

13. A _____ is an equation in which each term is either a constant or the product of a constant times the first power of a variable.
   a. Linear equation0
   b. Thing
   c. Undefined
   d. Undefined

14. _____ is a notation for writing numbers that is often used by scientists and mathematicians to make it easier to write large and small numbers.
   a. Scientific notation0
   b. Thing
   c. Undefined
   d. Undefined

15. In mathematics, a _____ is an expression that is constructed from one or more variables and constants, using only the operations of addition, subtraction, multiplication, and constant positive whole number exponents. is a _____. Note in particular that division by an expression containing a variable is not in general allowed in polynomials. [1]
   a. Thing
   b. Polynomial0
   c. Undefined
   d. Undefined

16. The mathematical concept of a _____ expresses the intuitive idea of deterministic dependence between two quantities, one of which is viewed as primary and the other as secondary. A _____ then is a way to associate a unique output for each input of a specified type, for example, a real number or an element of a given set.
   a. Thing
   b. Function0
   c. Undefined
   d. Undefined

17. An _____ is a combination of numbers, operators, grouping symbols and/or free variables and bound variables arranged in a meaningful way which can be evaluated..
   a. Expression0
   b. Thing
   c. Undefined
   d. Undefined

18. _____ has many meanings, most of which simply .
   a. Power0
   b. Thing
   c. Undefined
   d. Undefined

19. In mathematics, a subset of Euclidean space R^n is called _____ if it is closed and bounded.
   a. Thing
   b. Compact0
   c. Undefined
   d. Undefined

20. In mathematics, factorization (British English: factorisation) or factoring is the decomposition of an object (for example, a number, a polynomial, or a matrix) into a product of other objects, or _____, which when multiplied together give the original.
   a. Factors0
   b. Thing
   c. Undefined
   d. Undefined

Chapter 5. EXPONENTS, POLYNOMIALS, AND POLYNOMIAL FUNCTIONS

21. In mathematics, _____ growth occurs when the growth rate of a function is always proportional to the function's current size.
   a. Exponential0
   b. Thing
   c. Undefined
   d. Undefined

22. The _____ governs the differentiation of products of differentiable functions.
   a. Thing
   b. Product rule0
   c. Undefined
   d. Undefined

23. In mathematics, a _____ may be described informally as a number that can be given by an infinite decimal representation.
   a. Real number0
   b. Thing
   c. Undefined
   d. Undefined

24. A _____ is the result of the addition of a set of numbers. The numbers may be natural numbers, complex numbers, matrices, or still more complicated objects. An infinite _____ is a subtle procedure known as a series.
   a. Thing
   b. Sum0
   c. Undefined
   d. Undefined

25. The _____ are the only integral domain whose positive elements are well-ordered, and in which order is preserved by addition. Like the natural numbers, the _____ form a countably infinite set. The set of all _____ is usually denoted in mathematics by a boldface Z .
   a. Integers0
   b. Thing
   c. Undefined
   d. Undefined

26. In mathematics, _____ is an elementary arithmetic operation. When one of the numbers is a whole number, _____ is the repeated sum of the other number.
   a. Thing
   b. Multiplication0
   c. Undefined
   d. Undefined

27. _____, either of the curved-bracket punctuation marks that together make a set of _____
   a. Thing
   b. Parentheses0
   c. Undefined
   d. Undefined

28. In mathematics, a _____ is the end result of a division problem. It can also be expressed as the number of times the divisor divides into the dividend.
   a. Thing
   b. Quotient0
   c. Undefined
   d. Undefined

29. The _____ is a method of finding the derivative of a function that is the quotient of two other functions for which derivatives exist.
   a. Thing
   b. Quotient rule0
   c. Undefined
   d. Undefined

30. A _____ is a numeral used to indicate a count. The most common use of the word today is to name the part of a fraction that tells the number or count of equal parts.

Chapter 5. EXPONENTS, POLYNOMIALS, AND POLYNOMIAL FUNCTIONS

   a. Numerator0
   b. Thing
   c. Undefined
   d. Undefined

31. A _____ is the part of a fraction that tells how many equal parts make up a whole, and which is used in the name of the fraction: "halves", "thirds", "fourths" or "quarters", "fifths" and so on.
   a. Denominator0
   b. Concept
   c. Undefined
   d. Undefined

32. In geometry, a _____ (Greek words diairo = divide and metro = measure) of a circle is any straight line segment that passes through the centre and whose endpoints are on the circular boundary, or, in more modern usage, the length of such a line segment. When using the word in the more modern sense, one speaks of the _____ rather than a _____, because all diameters of a circle have the same length. This length is twice the radius. The _____ of a circle is also the longest chord that the circle has.
   a. Thing
   b. Diameter0
   c. Undefined
   d. Undefined

33. The decimal separator is a symbol used to mark the boundary between the integral and the fractional parts of a decimal numeral. Terms implying the symbol used are _____ and decimal comma.
   a. Decimal point0
   b. Concept
   c. Undefined
   d. Undefined

34. The _____, the average in everyday English, which is also called the arithmetic _____ (and is distinguished from the geometric _____ or harmonic _____). The average is also called the sample _____. The expected value of a random variable, which is also called the population _____.
   a. Mean0
   b. Thing
   c. Undefined
   d. Undefined

35. In mathematics, _____ is a part of the set theoretic notion of function.
   a. Thing
   b. Image0
   c. Undefined
   d. Undefined

36. _____ is the practice of doing mathematical calculations using only the human brain, with no help from any computing devices.
   a. Concept
   b. Mental math0
   c. Undefined
   d. Undefined

37. A _____ is a unit of length in the metric system, equal to one thousand metres, the current SI base unit of length
   a. Thing
   b. Kilometer0
   c. Undefined
   d. Undefined

38. The metre (or _____, see spelling differences) is a measure of length. It is the basic unit of length in the metric system and in the International System of Units (SI), used around the world for general and scientific purposes.
   a. Meter0
   b. Concept
   c. Undefined
   d. Undefined

39. _____ is a method for differentiating expressions involving exponentiation the power operation.

56 **Chapter 5. EXPONENTS, POLYNOMIALS, AND POLYNOMIAL FUNCTIONS**

 a. Power rule0
 b. Thing
 c. Undefined
 d. Undefined

40. The _____ of measurement are a globally standardized and modernized form of the metric system.
 a. Thing
 b. Units0
 c. Undefined
 d. Undefined

41. The _____ of a solid object is the three-dimensional concept of how much space it occupies, often quantified numerically.
 a. Thing
 b. Volume0
 c. Undefined
 d. Undefined

42. A _____ is a three-dimensional solid object bounded by six square faces, facets, or sides, with three meeting at each vertex.
 a. Cube0
 b. Thing
 c. Undefined
 d. Undefined

43. _____ are cubes in which all sides are of the same length and all face perpendicular to each other including an atom at each corner of the unigt cell.
 a. Cubic units0
 b. Thing
 c. Undefined
 d. Undefined

44. A _____ is a function that assigns a number to subsets of a given set.
 a. Thing
 b. Measure0
 c. Undefined
 d. Undefined

45. Equivalence is the condition of being _____ or essentially equal.
 a. Equivalent0
 b. Thing
 c. Undefined
 d. Undefined

46. _____ is the property of a physical object that quantifies the amount of matter and energy it is equivalent to.
 a. Thing
 b. Mass0
 c. Undefined
 d. Undefined

47. _____ is mass m per unit volume V.
 a. Thing
 b. Density0
 c. Undefined
 d. Undefined

48. In plane geometry, a _____ is a polygon with four equal sides, four right angles, and parallel opposite sides. In algebra, the _____ of a number is that number multiplied by itself.
 a. Square0
 b. Thing
 c. Undefined
 d. Undefined

49. In sociology and biology a _____ is the collection of people or organisms of a particular species living in a given geographic area or space, usually measured by a census.

Chapter 5. EXPONENTS, POLYNOMIALS, AND POLYNOMIAL FUNCTIONS 57

    a. Thing
    c. Undefined
    b. Population0
    d. Undefined

50. A _____ is a unit of length, usually used to measure distance, in a number of different systems, including Imperial units, United States customary units and Norwegian/Swedish mil. Its size can vary from system to system, but in each is between 1 and 10 kilometers. In contemporary English contexts _____ refers to either:
    a. Mile0
    c. Undefined
    b. Thing
    d. Undefined

51. A _____ is a four-sided plane figure that has two sets of opposite parallel sides.
    a. Concept
    c. Undefined
    b. Parallelogram0
    d. Undefined

52. In mathematics, an _____, mean, or central tendency of a data set refers to a measure of the "middle" or "expected" value of the data set.
    a. Concept
    c. Undefined
    b. Average0
    d. Undefined

53. In physics, _____ is an influence that may cause an object to accelerate. It may be experienced as a lift, a push, or a pull. The actual acceleration of the body is determined by the vector sum of all forces acting on it, known as net _____ or resultant _____.
    a. Thing
    c. Undefined
    b. Force0
    d. Undefined

54. A _____ is a symbolic representation denoting a quantity or expression. It often represents an "unknown" quantity that has the potential to change.
    a. Thing
    c. Undefined
    b. Variable0
    d. Undefined

55. In mathematics, a _____ is a particular kind of polynomial, having just one term.
    a. Monomial0
    c. Undefined
    b. Thing
    d. Undefined

56. In mathematics, there are several meanings of _____ depending on the subject.
    a. Thing
    c. Undefined
    b. Degree0
    d. Undefined

57. In elementary algebra, a _____ is a polynomial with two terms: the sum of two monomials. It is the simplest kind of polynomial except for a monomial.
    a. Binomial0
    c. Undefined
    b. Thing
    d. Undefined

58. In mathematics and the mathematical sciences, a _____ is a fixed, but possibly unspecified, value. This is in contrast to a variable, which is not fixed.

a. Thing
b. Constant0
c. Undefined
d. Undefined

59. The _____ is the sum of the exponents of the variables in the term.
    a. Thing
    b. Degree of a term0
    c. Undefined
    d. Undefined

60. In mathematics, a _____ is a constant multiplicative factor of a certain object. The object can be such things as a variable, a vector, a function, etc. For example, the _____ of $9x^2$ is 9.
    a. Thing
    b. Coefficient0
    c. Undefined
    d. Undefined

61. _____ is a fixed, but possibly unspecified, value. This is in contrast to a variable, which is not fixed.
    a. Thing
    b. Constant term0
    c. Undefined
    d. Undefined

62. In mathematics, a set is called _____ if there is a bijection between the set and some set of the form {1, 2, ..., n} where n is a natural number.
    a. Finite0
    b. Thing
    c. Undefined
    d. Undefined

63. The _____ is the maximum of the degrees of all terms in the polynomial.
    a. Degree of a polynomial0
    b. Thing
    c. Undefined
    d. Undefined

64. In mathematics, and in particular in abstract algebra, the _____ is a property of binary operations that generalises the distributive law from elementary algebra.
    a. Thing
    b. Distributive property0
    c. Undefined
    d. Undefined

65. The _____ is a property of multiplication or addition where the product or sum remains the same, regardless of whether or not the order of the addends or factors are changed.
    a. Commutative property0
    b. Thing
    c. Undefined
    d. Undefined

66. In mathematics, the additive inverse, or _____ of a number n is the number that, when added to n, yields zero. The additive inverse of n is denoted −n. For example, 7 is −7, because 7 + (−7) = 0, and the additive inverse of −0.3 is 0.3, because −0.3 + 0.3 = 0.
    a. Opposite0
    b. Thing
    c. Undefined
    d. Undefined

67. In mathematics, the _____ of a number n is the number that, when added to n, yields zero. The _____ of n is denoted −n. For example, 7 is −7, because 7 + (−7) = 0, and the _____ of −0.3 is 0.3, because −0.3 + 0.3 = 0.
    a. Additive inverse0
    b. Thing
    c. Undefined
    d. Undefined

Chapter 5. EXPONENTS, POLYNOMIALS, AND POLYNOMIAL FUNCTIONS

68. _____ are the basic objects of study in graph theory. Informally speaking, a graph is a set of objects called points, nodes, or vertices connected by links called lines or edges.
   a. Graphs0
   b. Thing
   c. Undefined
   d. Undefined

69. In common philosophical language, a proposition or _____, is the content of an assertion, that is, it is true-or-false and defined by the meaning of a particular piece of language.
   a. Concept
   b. Statement0
   c. Undefined
   d. Undefined

70. _____ of an object is its speed in a particular direction.
   a. Thing
   b. Velocity0
   c. Undefined
   d. Undefined

71. _____ is a set, with some particular properties and usually some additional structure, such as the operations of addition or multiplication, for instance.
   a. Space0
   b. Thing
   c. Undefined
   d. Undefined

72. _____, from Latin meaning "to make progress", is defined in two different ways. Pure economic _____ is the increase in wealth that an investor has from making an investment, taking into consideration all costs associated with that investment including the opportunity cost of capital.
   a. Profit0
   b. Thing
   c. Undefined
   d. Undefined

73. _____ is the level of functional and/or metabolic efficiency of an organism at both the micro level.
   a. Health0
   b. Thing
   c. Undefined
   d. Undefined

74. _____ is a kind of property which exists as magnitude or multitude. It is among the basic classes of things along with quality, substance, change, and relation.
   a. Amount0
   b. Thing
   c. Undefined
   d. Undefined

75. Initial objects are also called _____, and terminal objects are also called final.
   a. Coterminal0
   b. Thing
   c. Undefined
   d. Undefined

76. A _____ is any object propelled through space by the applicationp of a force.
   a. Projectile0
   b. Thing
   c. Undefined
   d. Undefined

77. _____ is the application of tools and a processing medium to the transformation of raw materials into finished goods for sale.

Chapter 5. EXPONENTS, POLYNOMIALS, AND POLYNOMIAL FUNCTIONS

   a. Thing
   b. Manufacturing0
   c. Undefined
   d. Undefined

78. _____ is a business term for the amount of money that a company receives from its activities in a given period, mostly from sales of products and/or services to customers
   a. Revenue0
   b. Thing
   c. Undefined
   d. Undefined

79. _____ is a synonym for information.
   a. Data0
   b. Thing
   c. Undefined
   d. Undefined

80. In geometry, the _____ of an object is a point in some sense in the middle of the object.
   a. Thing
   b. Center0
   c. Undefined
   d. Undefined

81. The _____ of an algebraic expression is the same equation, but without parentheses.
   a. Thing
   b. Expanded form0
   c. Undefined
   d. Undefined

82. In geometry, a _____ is defined as a quadrilateral where all four of its angles are right angles.
   a. Thing
   b. Rectangle0
   c. Undefined
   d. Undefined

83. In business, particularly accounting, a _____ is the time intervals that the accounts, statement, payments, or other calculations cover.
   a. Thing
   b. Period0
   c. Undefined
   d. Undefined

84. _____ also sometimes known as the double distributive property or more colloquially as foiling, is commonly taught to US high school students learning algebra as a mnemonic for remembering how to multiply two binomials polynomials with two terms.
   a. FOIL method0
   b. Thing
   c. Undefined
   d. Undefined

85. The _____ is commonly taught to US high school students learning algebra as a mnemonic for remembering how to multiply two binomials.
   a. FOIL rule0
   b. Thing
   c. Undefined
   d. Undefined

86. In Euclidean geometry, a _____ is the set of all points in a plane at a fixed distance, called the radius, from a given point, the center.
   a. Thing
   b. Circle0
   c. Undefined
   d. Undefined

Chapter 5. EXPONENTS, POLYNOMIALS, AND POLYNOMIAL FUNCTIONS

87. _____ is often used to describe the measurement of the steepness, incline, gradient, or grade of a straight line. The _____ is defined as the ratio of the "rise" divided by the "run" between two points on a line, or in other words, the ratio of the altitude change to the horizontal distance between any two points on the line.
   a. Slope0
   b. Thing
   c. Undefined
   d. Undefined

88. In mathematics, the _____ of two non-zero integers, is the largest positive integer that divides both numbers without remainder.
   a. Thing
   b. Greatest common divisor0
   c. Undefined
   d. Undefined

89. A _____ is a negotiable instrument instructing a financial institution to pay a specific amount of a specific currency from a specific demand account held in the maker/depositor's name with that institution. Both the maker and payee may be natural persons or legal entities.
   a. Thing
   b. Check0
   c. Undefined
   d. Undefined

90. In mathematics, the conjugate _____ or adjoint matrix of an m-by-n matrix A with complex entries is the n-by-m matrix A* obtained from A by taking the transpose and then taking the complex conjugate of each entry.
   a. Pairs0
   b. Thing
   c. Undefined
   d. Undefined

91. In classical geometry, a _____ of a circle or sphere is any line segment from its center to its boundary. By extension, the _____ of a circle or sphere is the length of any such segment. The _____ is half the diameter. In science and engineering the term _____ of curvature is commonly used as a synonym for _____.
   a. Radius0
   b. Thing
   c. Undefined
   d. Undefined

92. _____ is the difference of electrical potential between two points of an electrical or electronic circuit, expressed in volts
   a. Voltage0
   b. Thing
   c. Undefined
   d. Undefined

93. A _____ is a special kind of ratio, indicating a relationship between two measurements with different units, such as miles to gallons or cents to pounds.
   a. Thing
   b. Rate0
   c. Undefined
   d. Undefined

94. _____ is the fee paid on borrowed money.
   a. Thing
   b. Interest0
   c. Undefined
   d. Undefined

95. A _____ are accounts maintained by commercial banks, savings and loan associations, credit unions, and mutual savings banks that pay interest but can not be used directly as money by, for example, writing a cheque.

Chapter 5. EXPONENTS, POLYNOMIALS, AND POLYNOMIAL FUNCTIONS

    a. Thing
    c. Undefined
    b. Savings account0
    d. Undefined

96. In mathematics, a _____ number (or a _____) is a natural number that has exactly two (distinct) natural number divisors, which are 1 and the _____ number itself.
    a. Thing
    c. Undefined
    b. Prime0
    d. Undefined

97. In combinatorial mathematics, a _____ is an un-ordered collection of unique elements.
    a. Concept
    c. Undefined
    b. Combination0
    d. Undefined

98. The term _____ can refer to an integer which is the square of some other integer, or an algebraic expression that can be factored as the square of some other expression.
    a. Thing
    c. Undefined
    b. Perfect square0
    d. Undefined

99. In mathematics, a _____ can mean either an element of the set {1, 2, 3, ...} (i.e the positive integers) or an element of the set {0, 1, 2, 3, ...} (i.e. the non-negative integers).
    a. Whole number0
    c. Undefined
    b. Concept
    d. Undefined

100. In mathematics the _____ refers to the identity: $a^2 - b^2 = (a+b)(a-b)$
    a. Thing
    c. Undefined
    b. Difference of two squares0
    d. Undefined

101. _____ are of a number n in its third power-the result of multiplying it by itself three times.
    a. Thing
    c. Undefined
    b. Cubes0
    d. Undefined

102. In mathematics, a _____ is a polynomial equation of the second degree. The general form is $ax^2 + bx + c = 0$.
    a. Thing
    c. Undefined
    b. Quadratic equation0
    d. Undefined

103. A _____ is a vehicle, missile or aircraft which obtains thrust by the reaction to the ejection of fast moving fluid from within a _____ engine.
    a. Rocket0
    c. Undefined
    b. Thing
    d. Undefined

104. _____, in economics and political economy, are the distributions or payments awarded to the various suppliers of the factors of production.
    a. Returns0
    c. Undefined
    b. Thing
    d. Undefined

105. A _____ is one of the basic shapes of geometry: a polygon with three vertices and three sides which are straight line segments.

Chapter 5. EXPONENTS, POLYNOMIALS, AND POLYNOMIAL FUNCTIONS

a. Thing
b. Triangle0
c. Undefined
d. Undefined

106. In geometry and trigonometry, a _____ is defined as an angle between two straight intersecting lines of ninety degrees, or one-quarter of a circle.
a. Thing
b. Right angle0
c. Undefined
d. Undefined

107. _____ has one 90° internal angle a right angle.
a. Thing
b. Right triangle0
c. Undefined
d. Undefined

108. In mathematics, a _____ is a statement that can be proved on the basis of explicitly stated or previously agreed assumptions.
a. Thing
b. Theorem0
c. Undefined
d. Undefined

109. The _____ of a right triangle is the triangle's longest side; the side opposite the right angle.
a. Thing
b. Hypotenuse0
c. Undefined
d. Undefined

110. In a right triangle, the _____ of the triangle are the two sides that are perpendicular to each other, as opposed to the hypotenuse.
a. Legs0
b. Thing
c. Undefined
d. Undefined

111. _____ is a relation in Euclidean geometry among the three sides of a right triangle.
a. Pythagorean Theorem0
b. Thing
c. Undefined
d. Undefined

112. _____ means in succession or back-to-back
a. Consecutive0
b. Thing
c. Undefined
d. Undefined

113. A _____ can refer to a line joining two nonadjacent vertices of a polygon or polyhedron, or in some contexts any upward or downward sloping line. .
a. Diagonal0
b. Thing
c. Undefined
d. Undefined

114. In mathematics, the _____ f is the collection of all ordered pairs . In particular, graph means the graphical representation of this collection, in the form of a curve or surface, together with axes, etc. Graphing on a Cartesian plane is sometimes referred to as curve sketching.
a. Graph of a function0
b. Thing
c. Undefined
d. Undefined

Chapter 5. EXPONENTS, POLYNOMIALS, AND POLYNOMIAL FUNCTIONS

115. In geographic information systems, a _____ comprises an entity with a geographic location, typically determined by points, arcs, or polygons. Carriageways and cadastres exemplify _____ data.
    a. Feature0
    b. Thing
    c. Undefined
    d. Undefined

116. André-_____ Ampère was a French physicist who is generally credited as one of the main discoverers of electromagnetism.
    a. Person
    b. Marie0
    c. Undefined
    d. Undefined

117. In mathematics, a _____ or rhodonea curve is a sinusoid plotted in polar coordinates.
    a. Rose0
    b. Thing
    c. Undefined
    d. Undefined

118. Any point where a graph makes contact with an coordinate axis is called an _____ of the graph
    a. Intercept0
    b. Thing
    c. Undefined
    d. Undefined

119. In geometry, a _____ is a special kind of point, usually a corner of a polygon, polyhedron, or higher dimensional polytope. In the geometry of curves a _____ is a point of where the first derivative of curvature is zero. In graph theory, a _____ is the fundamental unit out of which graphs are formed
    a. Vertex0
    b. Thing
    c. Undefined
    d. Undefined

120. In mathematics, the _____ is a conic section generated by the intersection of a right circular conical surface and a plane parallel to a generating straight line of that surface. It can also be defined as locus of points in a plane which are equidistant from a given point.
    a. Thing
    b. Parabola0
    c. Undefined
    d. Undefined

121. A _____ is a first degree polynomial mathematical function of the form: f(x) = mx + b where m and b are real constants and x is a real variable.
    a. Linear function0
    b. Thing
    c. Undefined
    d. Undefined

122. In mathematics, the _____ of a function is the set of all "output" values produced by that function. Given a function $f : A \to B$, the _____ of f, is defined to be the set {x ∈ B:x=f(a) for some a ∈ A}.
    a. Range0
    b. Thing
    c. Undefined
    d. Undefined

123. In elementary algebra, an _____ is a set that contains every real number between two indicated numbers and may contain the two numbers themselves.
    a. Thing
    b. Interval0
    c. Undefined
    d. Undefined

Chapter 5. EXPONENTS, POLYNOMIALS, AND POLYNOMIAL FUNCTIONS

124. _____ is the notation in which permitted values for a variable are expressed as ranging over a certain interval; "5 < x < 9" is an example of the application of _____.
 a. Thing
 b. Interval notation0
 c. Undefined
 d. Undefined

125. In mathematics, a _____ of a k-place relation $L \subseteq X_1 \times ... \times X_k$ is one of the sets X_j, $1 \le j \le k$. In the special case where k = 2 and $L \subseteq X_1 \times X_2$ is a function $L : X_1 \to X_2$, it is conventional to refer to X_1 as the _____ of the function and to refer to X_2 as the codomain of the function.
 a. Thing
 b. Domain0
 c. Undefined
 d. Undefined

126. In mathematics, an inequality is a statement about the relative size or order of two objects. For example 14 > 10, or 14 is _____ 10.
 a. Thing
 b. Greater than0
 c. Undefined
 d. Undefined

127. In mathematics, the concept of a _____ tries to capture the intuitive idea of a geometrical one-dimensional and continuous object. A simple example is the circle.
 a. Thing
 b. Curve0
 c. Undefined
 d. Undefined

128. An _____ is a collection of two not necessarily distinct objects, one of which is distinguished as the first coordinate and the other as the second coordinate.
 a. Thing
 b. Ordered pair0
 c. Undefined
 d. Undefined

129. _____ is a test to determine if a relation or its graph is a function or not
 a. Thing
 b. Vertical line test0
 c. Undefined
 d. Undefined

130. Acid _____ ratio measures the ability of a company to use its near cash or quick assets to immediately extinguish its current liabilities.
 a. Thing
 b. Test0
 c. Undefined
 d. Undefined

131. A _____ is a polynomial function of the form $f(x) = ax^2 + bx + c$, where a, b, c are real numbers and a , 0.
 a. Quadratic function0
 b. Event
 c. Undefined
 d. Undefined

132. The _____ of a ring *R* is defined to be the smallest positive integer *n* such that *n* a = 0, for all a in R.
 a. Thing
 b. Characteristic0
 c. Undefined
 d. Undefined

133. _____ means "constancy", i.e. if something retains a certain feature even after we change a way of looking at it, then it is symmetric.

Chapter 5. EXPONENTS, POLYNOMIALS, AND POLYNOMIAL FUNCTIONS

   a. Symmetry0
   b. Thing
   c. Undefined
   d. Undefined

134. An _____ is a straight line around which a geometric figure can be rotated.
   a. Axis0
   b. Thing
   c. Undefined
   d. Undefined

135. _____ of a two-dimensional figure is a line such that, if a perpendicular is constructed, any two points lying on the perpendicular at equal distances from the _____ are identical.
   a. Axis of symmetry0
   b. Thing
   c. Undefined
   d. Undefined

136. The easiest _____ prime numbers resides in the use of the Sieve of Eratosthenes, an algorithm that discovers all prime numbers to a specified integer.
   a. Thing
   b. Method for finding0
   c. Undefined
   d. Undefined

137. _____ is a function of the form
   a. Thing
   b. Cubic function0
   c. Undefined
   d. Undefined

138. An _____ of a product of sums expresses it as a sum of products by using the fact that multiplication distributes over addition.
   a. Thing
   b. Expansion0
   c. Undefined
   d. Undefined

139. _____ is a physical property of a system that underlies the common notions of hot and cold; something that is hotter has the greater _____.
   a. Thing
   b. Temperature0
   c. Undefined
   d. Undefined

140. In mathematics, a _____ is any one of several different types of functions, mappings, operations, or transformations.
   a. Thing
   b. Projection0
   c. Undefined
   d. Undefined

141. _____ is the interdisciplinary scientific study of the atmosphere that focuses on weather processes and forecasting.
   a. Meteorology0
   b. Thing
   c. Undefined
   d. Undefined

142. The _____ integers are all the integers from zero on upwards.
   a. Nonnegative0
   b. Thing
   c. Undefined
   d. Undefined

Chapter 5. EXPONENTS, POLYNOMIALS, AND POLYNOMIAL FUNCTIONS

143. A _____ is a set of numbers that designate location in a given reference system, such as x,y in a planar _____ system or an x,y,z in a three-dimensional _____ system.
    a. Thing
    b. Coordinate0
    c. Undefined
    d. Undefined

144. _____ is the distance around a given two-dimensional object. As a general rule, the _____ of a polygon can always be calculated by adding all the length of the sides together. So, the formula for triangles is P = a + b + c, where a, b and c stand for each side of it. For quadrilaterals the equation is P = a + b + c + d. For equilateral polygons, P = na, where n is the number of sides and a is the side length.
    a. Perimeter0
    b. Thing
    c. Undefined
    d. Undefined

145. In mathematics, a _____ of a complex-valued function f is a member x of the domain of f such that f(x) vanishes at x, that is, x : f (x) = 0.
    a. Root0
    b. Thing
    c. Undefined
    d. Undefined

146. The _____ is used to discard one of the variables in an equation, only to replace it with the actual value when solving multiple equations.
    a. Substitution method0
    b. Thing
    c. Undefined
    d. Undefined

147. In mathematics, in the field of group theory, a _____ of a group is a quasisimple subnormal subgroup.
    a. Component0
    b. Concept
    c. Undefined
    d. Undefined

148. In set theory and its applications throughout mathematics, _____ are a collection of sets (or sometimes other mathematical objects) that can be unambiguously defined by a property that all its members share.
    a. Thing
    b. Classes0
    c. Undefined
    d. Undefined

Chapter 6. RATIONAL EXPRESSIONS

1. _____ forms part of thinking. Considered the most complex of all intellectual functions, _____ has been defined as higher-order cognitive process that requires the modulation and control of more routine or fundamental skills.
   a. Thing
   b. Problem solving0
   c. Undefined
   d. Undefined

2. In mathematics, _____ expressions is used to reduce the expression into the lowest possible term.
   a. Simplifying0
   b. Thing
   c. Undefined
   d. Undefined

3. In mathematics, a _____ number is a number which can be expressed as a ratio of two integers. Non-integer _____ numbers (commonly called fractions) are usually written as the vulgar fraction a / b, where b is not zero.
   a. Thing
   b. Rational0
   c. Undefined
   d. Undefined

4. In mathematics, a _____ is any function which can be written as the ratio of two polynomial functions.
   a. Rational function0
   b. Thing
   c. Undefined
   d. Undefined

5. _____ or arithmetics is the oldest and most elementary branch of mathematics, used by almost everyone, for tasks ranging from simple daily counting to advanced science and business calculations.
   a. Arithmetic0
   b. Thing
   c. Undefined
   d. Undefined

6. An _____ is a combination of numbers, operators, grouping symbols and/or free variables and bound variables arranged in a meaningful way which can be evaluated..
   a. Expression0
   b. Thing
   c. Undefined
   d. Undefined

7. The _____ are the only integral domain whose positive elements are well-ordered, and in which order is preserved by addition. Like the natural numbers, the _____ form a countably infinite set. The set of all _____ is usually denoted in mathematics by a boldface Z .
   a. Integers0
   b. Thing
   c. Undefined
   d. Undefined

8. A _____ is the part of the dividend that is left over when the dividend is not evenly divisible by the divisor.
   a. Thing
   b. Remainder0
   c. Undefined
   d. Undefined

9. _____ is a branch of mathematics concerning the study of structure, relation and quantity.
   a. Algebra0
   b. Concept
   c. Undefined
   d. Undefined

10. In mathematics, _____ allows the rapid division of any polynomial by a binomial of the form x − r. It was described by Paolo Ruffini in 1809. _____ is a special case of long division when the divisor is a linear factor.
    a. Thing
    b. Ruffini's rule0
    c. Undefined
    d. Undefined

Chapter 6. RATIONAL EXPRESSIONS

11. In mathematics, a _____ is an expression that is constructed from one or more variables and constants, using only the operations of addition, subtraction, multiplication, and constant positive whole number exponents. is a _____. Note in particular that division by an expression containing a variable is not in general allowed in polynomials. [1]
    a. Thing
    b. Polynomial0
    c. Undefined
    d. Undefined

12. The mathematical concept of a _____ expresses the intuitive idea of deterministic dependence between two quantities, one of which is viewed as primary and the other as secondary. A _____ then is a way to associate a unique output for each input of a specified type, for example, a real number or an element of a given set.
    a. Thing
    b. Function0
    c. Undefined
    d. Undefined

13. In mathematics, defined and _____ are used to explain whether or not expressions have meaningful, sensible, and unambiguous values.
    a. Undefined0
    b. Thing
    c. Undefined
    d. Undefined

14. In mathematics, a subset of Euclidean space R^n is called _____ if it is closed and bounded.
    a. Compact0
    b. Thing
    c. Undefined
    d. Undefined

15. A _____ is a symbolic representation denoting a quantity or expression. It often represents an "unknown" quantity that has the potential to change.
    a. Thing
    b. Variable0
    c. Undefined
    d. Undefined

16. A _____ is the part of a fraction that tells how many equal parts make up a whole, and which is used in the name of the fraction: "halves", "thirds", "fourths" or "quarters", "fifths" and so on.
    a. Denominator0
    b. Concept
    c. Undefined
    d. Undefined

17. In mathematics, a _____ of a k-place relation $L \subseteq X_1 \times ... \times X_k$ is one of the sets X_j, $1 \leq j \leq k$. In the special case where k = 2 and $L \subseteq X_1 \times X_2$ is a function $L : X_1 \to X_2$, it is conventional to refer to X_1 as the _____ of the function and to refer to X_2 as the codomain of the function.
    a. Thing
    b. Domain0
    c. Undefined
    d. Undefined

18. A _____ signifies a point or points of probability on a subject e.g., the _____ of creativity, which allows for the formation of rule or norm or law by interpretation of the phenomena events that can be created.
    a. Principle0
    b. Thing
    c. Undefined
    d. Undefined

19. A _____ is a numeral used to indicate a count. The most common use of the word today is to name the part of a fraction that tells the number or count of equal parts.

Chapter 6. RATIONAL EXPRESSIONS

    a. Thing
    c. Undefined
    b. Numerator0
    d. Undefined

20. In mathematics, a _____ may be described informally as a number that can be given by an infinite decimal representation.
    a. Real number0
    b. Thing
    c. Undefined
    d. Undefined

21. _____ is the largest positive integer that divides both numbers without remainder.
    a. Common Factor0
    b. Thing
    c. Undefined
    d. Undefined

22. In mathematics, factorization (British English: factorisation) or factoring is the decomposition of an object (for example, a number, a polynomial, or a matrix) into a product of other objects, or _____, which when multiplied together give the original.
    a. Factors0
    b. Thing
    c. Undefined
    d. Undefined

23. In mathematics, the additive inverse, or _____ of a number n is the number that, when added to n, yields zero. The additive inverse of n is denoted −n. For example, 7 is −7, because 7 + (−7) = 0, and the additive inverse of −0.3 is 0.3, because −0.3 + 0.3 = 0.
    a. Thing
    b. Opposite0
    c. Undefined
    d. Undefined

24. In mathematics, a _____ is the result of multiplying, or an expression that identifies factors to be multiplied.
    a. Product0
    b. Thing
    c. Undefined
    d. Undefined

25. In mathematics, the multiplicative inverse of a number x, denoted 1/x or x^{-1}, is the number which, when multiplied by x, yields 1. The multiplicative inverse of x is also called the _____ of x.
    a. Thing
    b. Reciprocal0
    c. Undefined
    d. Undefined

26. In mathematics, a _____ is a number which can be expressed as a ratio of two integers. Non-integer rational numbers (commonly called fractions) are usually written as the vulgar fraction a / b, where b is not zero.
    a. Rational Number0
    b. Concept
    c. Undefined
    d. Undefined

27. In mathematics, _____ is an elementary arithmetic operation. When one of the numbers is a whole number, _____ is the repeated sum of the other number.
    a. Thing
    b. Multiplication0
    c. Undefined
    d. Undefined

28. _____ has many meanings, most of which simply .

Chapter 6. RATIONAL EXPRESSIONS

a. Thing
b. Power0
c. Undefined
d. Undefined

29. In mathematics, the concept of a _____ tries to capture the intuitive idea of a geometrical one-dimensional and continuous object. A simple example is the circle.
a. Thing
b. Curve0
c. Undefined
d. Undefined

30. In statistics, _____ means the most frequent value assumed by a random variable, or occurring in a sampling of a random variable.
a. Mode0
b. Concept
c. Undefined
d. Undefined

31. _____ is a test to determine if a relation or its graph is a function or not
a. Vertical line test0
b. Thing
c. Undefined
d. Undefined

32. Acid _____ ratio measures the ability of a company to use its near cash or quick assets to immediately extinguish its current liabilities.
a. Test0
b. Thing
c. Undefined
d. Undefined

33. In geographic information systems, a _____ comprises an entity with a geographic location, typically determined by points, arcs, or polygons. Carriageways and cadastres exemplify _____ data.
a. Feature0
b. Thing
c. Undefined
d. Undefined

34. A _____ is one of the basic shapes of geometry: a polygon with three vertices and three sides which are straight line segments.
a. Triangle0
b. Thing
c. Undefined
d. Undefined

35. The metre (or _____, see spelling differences) is a measure of length. It is the basic unit of length in the metric system and in the International System of Units (SI), used around the world for general and scientific purposes.
a. Concept
b. Meter0
c. Undefined
d. Undefined

36. A _____ is a four-sided plane figure that has two sets of opposite parallel sides.
a. Parallelogram0
b. Concept
c. Undefined
d. Undefined

37. The _____ is a popular form of gambling which involves the drawing of lots for a prize. Some governments forbid it, while others endorse it to the extent of organizign a national _____
a. Thing
b. Lottery0
c. Undefined
d. Undefined

Chapter 6. RATIONAL EXPRESSIONS

38. _____ is a kind of property which exists as magnitude or multitude. It is among the basic classes of things along with quality, substance, change, and relation.
   a. Thing
   b. Amount0
   c. Undefined
   d. Undefined

39. _____ is a way of expressing a number as a fraction of 100 per cent meaning "per hundred".
   a. Percent0
   b. Thing
   c. Undefined
   d. Undefined

40. _____ is a business term for the amount of money that a company receives from its activities in a given period, mostly from sales of products and/or services to customers
   a. Thing
   b. Revenue0
   c. Undefined
   d. Undefined

41. A _____ is the result of the addition of a set of numbers. The numbers may be natural numbers, complex numbers, matrices, or still more complicated objects. An infinite _____ is a subtle procedure known as a series.
   a. Sum0
   b. Thing
   c. Undefined
   d. Undefined

42. _____, either of the curved-bracket punctuation marks that together make a set of _____
   a. Thing
   b. Parentheses0
   c. Undefined
   d. Undefined

43. Equivalence is the condition of being _____ or essentially equal.
   a. Equivalent0
   b. Thing
   c. Undefined
   d. Undefined

44. In mathematics, there are several meanings of _____ depending on the subject.
   a. Thing
   b. Degree0
   c. Undefined
   d. Undefined

45. In mathematics, the _____ of a number n is the number that, when added to n, yields zero. The _____ of n is denoted −n. For example, 7 is −7, because 7 + (−7) = 0, and the _____ of −0.3 is 0.3, because −0.3 + 0.3 = 0.
   a. Additive inverse0
   b. Thing
   c. Undefined
   d. Undefined

46. In mathematics, a _____ of a complex-valued function f is a member x of the domain of f such that f(x) vanishes at x, that is, x : f (x) = 0.
   a. Thing
   b. Root0
   c. Undefined
   d. Undefined

47. _____ is a relation in Euclidean geometry among the three sides of a right triangle.
   a. Thing
   b. Pythagorean Theorem0
   c. Undefined
   d. Undefined

48. _____ has one 90° internal angle a right angle.

Chapter 6. RATIONAL EXPRESSIONS

    a. Right triangle0
    b. Thing
    c. Undefined
    d. Undefined

49. In mathematics, a _____ is a statement that can be proved on the basis of explicitly stated or previously agreed assumptions.
    a. Theorem0
    b. Thing
    c. Undefined
    d. Undefined

50. _____ is a mathematical operation, written a^n, involving two numbers, the base a and the exponent n.
    a. Exponentiating0
    b. Thing
    c. Undefined
    d. Undefined

51. _____ is a mathematical operation, written a^n, involving two numbers, the base a and the exponent n.
    a. Exponentiation0
    b. Thing
    c. Undefined
    d. Undefined

52. The _____ is the change in frequency and wavelength of a wave that is perceived by an observer moving relative to the source of the waves
    a. Thing
    b. Doppler Effect0
    c. Undefined
    d. Undefined

53. In mathematics, a _____ is the end result of a division problem. It can also be expressed as the number of times the divisor divides into the dividend.
    a. Quotient0
    b. Thing
    c. Undefined
    d. Undefined

54. _____ is a mathematical subject that includes the study of limits, derivatives, integrals, and power series and constitutes a major part of modern university curriculum.
    a. Calculus0
    b. Thing
    c. Undefined
    d. Undefined

55. The function difference divided by the point difference is known as the _____
    a. Thing
    b. Difference quotient0
    c. Undefined
    d. Undefined

56. In mathematics, a _____ is a particular kind of polynomial, having just one term.
    a. Thing
    b. Monomial0
    c. Undefined
    d. Undefined

57. A _____ is a negotiable instrument instructing a financial institution to pay a specific amount of a specific currency from a specific demand account held in the maker/depositor's name with that institution. Both the maker and payee may be natural persons or legal entities.
    a. Thing
    b. Check0
    c. Undefined
    d. Undefined

58. _____ is a payment made by a company to its shareholders

Chapter 6. RATIONAL EXPRESSIONS

a. Thing
b. Dividend0
c. Undefined
d. Undefined

59. In mathematics, a _____ of an integer n, also called a factor of n, is an integer which evenly divides n without leaving a remainder.
a. Divisor0
b. Thing
c. Undefined
d. Undefined

60. In arithmetic, _____ is a procedure for calculating the division of one integer, called the dividend, by another integer called the divisor, to produce a result called the quotient.
a. Thing
b. Long division0
c. Undefined
d. Undefined

61. In geometry, a _____ is defined as a quadrilateral where all four of its angles are right angles.
a. Thing
b. Rectangle0
c. Undefined
d. Undefined

62. In plane geometry, a _____ is a polygon with four equal sides, four right angles, and parallel opposite sides. In algebra, the _____ of a number is that number multiplied by itself.
a. Square0
b. Thing
c. Undefined
d. Undefined

63. In mathematics, a _____ function in the sense of algebraic geometry is an everywhere-defined, polynomial function on an algebraic variety V with values in the field K over which V is defined.
a. Regular0
b. Thing
c. Undefined
d. Undefined

64. A _____ is a polygon with six edges and six vertices.
a. Thing
b. Hexagon0
c. Undefined
d. Undefined

65. _____ is the distance around a given two-dimensional object. As a general rule, the _____ of a polygon can always be calculated by adding all the length of the sides together. So, the formula for triangles is P = a + b + c, where a, b and c stand for each side of it. For quadrilaterals the equation is P = a + b + c + d. For equilateral polygons, P = na, where n is the number of sides and a is the side length.
a. Thing
b. Perimeter0
c. Undefined
d. Undefined

66. A _____ is a unit of length, usually used to measure distance, in a number of different systems, including Imperial units, United States customary units and Norwegian/Swedish mil. Its size can vary from system to system, but in each is between 1 and 10 kilometers. In contemporary English contexts _____ refers to either:
a. Mile0
b. Thing
c. Undefined
d. Undefined

Chapter 6. RATIONAL EXPRESSIONS

67. In mathematics and logic, a _____ proof is a way of showing the truth or falsehood of a given statement by a straightforward combination of established facts, usually existing lemmas and theorems, without making any further assumptions.
    a. Direct0
    b. Thing
    c. Undefined
    d. Undefined

68. In topology and related areas of mathematics a _____ or Moore-Smith sequence is a generalization of a sequence, intended to unify the various notions of limit and generalize them to arbitrary topological spaces.
    a. Net0
    b. Thing
    c. Undefined
    d. Undefined

69. _____ is an accounting term which is commonly used in business.
    a. Net profit0
    b. Thing
    c. Undefined
    d. Undefined

70. _____, from Latin meaning "to make progress", is defined in two different ways. Pure economic _____ is the increase in wealth that an investor has from making an investment, taking into consideration all costs associated with that investment including the opportunity cost of capital.
    a. Profit0
    b. Thing
    c. Undefined
    d. Undefined

71. A _____ is a quantity that denotes the proportional amount or magnitude of one quantity relative to another.
    a. Ratio0
    b. Thing
    c. Undefined
    d. Undefined

72. In finance, a _____ is collateral that the holder of a position in securities, options, or futures contracts has to deposit to cover the credit risk of his counterparty.
    a. Margin0
    b. Thing
    c. Undefined
    d. Undefined

73. In common philosophical language, a proposition or _____, is the content of an assertion, that is, it is true-or-false and defined by the meaning of a particular piece of language.
    a. Concept
    b. Statement0
    c. Undefined
    d. Undefined

74. _____ in algebra is an application of polynomial long division.
    a. Thing
    b. Remainder theorem0
    c. Undefined
    d. Undefined

75. In elementary algebra, a _____ is a polynomial with two terms: the sum of two monomials. It is the simplest kind of polynomial except for a monomial.
    a. Binomial0
    b. Thing
    c. Undefined
    d. Undefined

76. In mathematics, a _____ is a constant multiplicative factor of a certain object. The object can be such things as a variable, a vector, a function, etc. For example, the _____ of $9x^2$ is 9.

Chapter 6. RATIONAL EXPRESSIONS

   a. Coefficient0
   b. Thing
   c. Undefined
   d. Undefined

77. In mathematics, a matrix can be thought of as each row or _____ being a vector. Hence, a space formed by row vectors or _____ vectors are said to be a row space or a _____ space.
   a. Concept
   b. Column0
   c. Undefined
   d. Undefined

78. The _____ of a solid object is the three-dimensional concept of how much space it occupies, often quantified numerically.
   a. Volume0
   b. Thing
   c. Undefined
   d. Undefined

79. The word _____ comes from the Latin word linearis, which means created by lines.
   a. Thing
   b. Linear0
   c. Undefined
   d. Undefined

80. In mathematics, and in particular in abstract algebra, the _____ is a property of binary operations that generalises the distributive law from elementary algebra.
   a. Distributive property0
   b. Thing
   c. Undefined
   d. Undefined

81. _____ means in succession or back-to-back
   a. Thing
   b. Consecutive0
   c. Undefined
   d. Undefined

82. _____ is a mathematical science pertaining to the collection, analysis, interpretation or explanation, and presentation of data. It is applicable to a wide variety of academic disciplines, from the physical and social sciences to the humanities.
   a. Thing
   b. Statistics0
   c. Undefined
   d. Undefined

83. In abstract algebra, _____ consists of sets with binary operations that satisfy certain axioms.
   a. Grouping0
   b. Thing
   c. Undefined
   d. Undefined

84. _____ are objects, characters, or other concrete representations of ideas, concepts, or other abstractions.
   a. Thing
   b. Symbols0
   c. Undefined
   d. Undefined

85. Two mathematical objects are equal if and only if they are precisely the same in every way. This defines a binary relation, _____, denoted by the sign of _____ "=" in such a way that the statement "x = y" means that x and y are equal.
   a. Equality0
   b. Thing
   c. Undefined
   d. Undefined

Chapter 6. RATIONAL EXPRESSIONS

86. _____ is electromagnetic radiation with a wavelength that is visible to the eye (visible _____) or, in a technical or scientific context, electromagnetic radiation of any wavelength.
   a. Thing
   b. Light0
   c. Undefined
   d. Undefined

87. In geometry, an _____ of a triangle is a straight line through a vertex and perpendicular to (i.e. forming a right angle with) the opposite side or an extension of the opposite side.
   a. Altitude0
   b. Concept
   c. Undefined
   d. Undefined

88. _____ are a measure of time.
   a. Thing
   b. Minutes0
   c. Undefined
   d. Undefined

89. In mathematics, a _____ is a two-dimensional manifold or surface that is perfectly flat.
   a. Thing
   b. Plane0
   c. Undefined
   d. Undefined

90. _____ is the transport of people on a trip/journey or the process or time involved in a person or object moving from one location to another.
   a. Thing
   b. Travel0
   c. Undefined
   d. Undefined

91. A _____ is a special kind of ratio, indicating a relationship between two measurements with different units, such as miles to gallons or cents to pounds.
   a. Rate0
   b. Thing
   c. Undefined
   d. Undefined

92. In mathematics and the mathematical sciences, a _____ is a fixed, but possibly unspecified, value. This is in contrast to a variable, which is not fixed.
   a. Constant0
   b. Thing
   c. Undefined
   d. Undefined

93. U.S. liquid _____ is legally defined as 231 cubic inches, and is equal to 3.785411784 litres or abotu 0.13368 cubic feet. This is the most common definition of a _____. The U.S. fluid ounce is defined as 1/128 of a U.S. _____.
   a. Gallon0
   b. Thing
   c. Undefined
   d. Undefined

94. A _____ is a numerical performance objective.
   a. Thing
   b. Quota0
   c. Undefined
   d. Undefined

95. Initial objects are also called _____, and terminal objects are also called final.

Chapter 6. RATIONAL EXPRESSIONS

a. Coterminal0
b. Thing
c. Undefined
d. Undefined

96. _____ is the design, analysis, and/or construction of works for practical purposes.
   a. Engineering0
   b. Thing
   c. Undefined
   d. Undefined

97. A _____ is a form of periodic payment from an employer to an employee, which is specified in an employment contract.
   a. Thing
   b. Salary0
   c. Undefined
   d. Undefined

98. A _____ is a landform that extends above the surrounding terrain in a limited area. A _____ is generally steeper than a hill, but there is no universally accepted standard definition for the height of a _____ or a hill although a _____ usually has an identifiable summit.
   a. Thing
   b. Mountain0
   c. Undefined
   d. Undefined

99. _____ is a unit of speed, expressing the number of international miles covered per hour.
   a. Miles per hour0
   b. Thing
   c. Undefined
   d. Undefined

100. The word _____ is used in a variety of ways in mathematics.
   a. Thing
   b. Index0
   c. Undefined
   d. Undefined

101. _____, Greek for "knowledge of nature," is the branch of science concerned with the discovery and characterization of universal laws which govern matter, energy, space, and time.
   a. Physics0
   b. Thing
   c. Undefined
   d. Undefined

102. In classical geometry, a _____ of a circle or sphere is any line segment from its center to its boundary. By extension, the _____ of a circle or sphere is the length of any such segment. The _____ is half the diameter. In science and engineering the term _____ of curvature is commonly used as a synonym for _____.
   a. Thing
   b. Radius0
   c. Undefined
   d. Undefined

103. The _____ is the distance around a closed curve. _____ is a kind of perimeter.
   a. Thing
   b. Circumference0
   c. Undefined
   d. Undefined

104. In mathematics, two quantities are called _____ if they vary in such a way that one of the quantities is a constant multiple of the other, or equivalently if they have a constant ratio.
   a. Thing
   b. Proportional0
   c. Undefined
   d. Undefined

Chapter 6. RATIONAL EXPRESSIONS

105. _____ is a special mathematical relationship between two quantities. Two quantities are called proportional if they vary in such a way that one of the quantities is a constant multiple of the other, or equivalently if they have a constant ratio.
   a. Thing
   b. Proportionality0
   c. Undefined
   d. Undefined

106. _____ is the relationship between two variables, like a ratio in which the two quantities being compared are different units.
   a. Thing
   b. Direct variation0
   c. Undefined
   d. Undefined

107. _____ is often used to describe the measurement of the steepness, incline, gradient, or grade of a straight line. The _____ is defined as the ratio of the "rise" divided by the "run" between two points on a line, or in other words, the ratio of the altitude change to the horizontal distance between any two points on the line.
   a. Slope0
   b. Thing
   c. Undefined
   d. Undefined

108. In mathematics, the _____ of a coordinate system is the point where the axes of the system intersect.
   a. Thing
   b. Origin0
   c. Undefined
   d. Undefined

109. The _____ of measurement are a globally standardized and modernized form of the metric system.
   a. Units0
   b. Thing
   c. Undefined
   d. Undefined

110. An _____ is a straight line around which a geometric figure can be rotated.
   a. Axis0
   b. Thing
   c. Undefined
   d. Undefined

111. In astronomy, geography, geometry and related sciences and contexts, a plane is said to be _____ at a given point if it is locally perpendicular to the gradient of the gravity field, i.e., with the direction of the gravitational force at that point.
   a. Horizontal0
   b. Thing
   c. Undefined
   d. Undefined

112. _____ element of an element x with respect to a binary operation * with identity element e is an element y such that x * y = y * x = e. In particular,
   a. Inverse0
   b. Thing
   c. Undefined
   d. Undefined

113. _____ is a relationship among three or more variables in which each pair of variables varies directly or inversely.
   a. Joint variation0
   b. Thing
   c. Undefined
   d. Undefined

114. In mathematics, a _____ is a quadric surface, with the following equation in Cartesian coordinates: $(x/_a)^2 + (y/_b)^2 = 1$.

Chapter 6. RATIONAL EXPRESSIONS

    a. Thing   b. Cylinder0
    c. Undefined   d. Undefined

115. A _____ of a number is the product of that number with any integer.
    a. Thing   b. Multiple0
    c. Undefined   d. Undefined

116. In geometry, a _____ (Greek words diairo = divide and metro = measure) of a circle is any straight line segment that passes through the centre and whose endpoints are on the circular boundary, or, in more modern usage, the length of such a line segment. When using the word in the more modern sense, one speaks of the _____ rather than a _____, because all diameters of a circle have the same length. This length is twice the radius. The _____ of a circle is also the longest chord that the circle has.
    a. Thing   b. Diameter0
    c. Undefined   d. Undefined

117. The _____ of a geographic location is its height above a fixed reference point, often the mean sea level.
    a. Elevation0   b. Thing
    c. Undefined   d. Undefined

118. In mathematics, a _____ of a number x is a number r such that r^2 = x, or in words, a number r whose square (the result of multiplying the number by itself) is x.
    a. Square root0   b. Thing
    c. Undefined   d. Undefined

119. In sociology and biology a _____ is the collection of people or organisms of a particular species living in a given geographic area or space, usually measured by a census.
    a. Population0   b. Thing
    c. Undefined   d. Undefined

120. _____ is a physical property of a system that underlies the common notions of hot and cold; something that is hotter has the greater _____.
    a. Thing   b. Temperature0
    c. Undefined   d. Undefined

121. In geometry, the _____ of an object is a point in some sense in the middle of the object.
    a. Thing   b. Center0
    c. Undefined   d. Undefined

122. _____ is the difference of electrical potential between two points of an electrical or electronic circuit, expressed in volts
    a. Voltage0   b. Thing
    c. Undefined   d. Undefined

123. The _____, in practice often shortened to amp, is a unit of electric current, or amount of electric charge per second.

Chapter 6. RATIONAL EXPRESSIONS

    a. Thing
    c. Undefined
    b. Amperes0
    d. Undefined

124. A _____ is a three-dimensional solid object bounded by six square faces, facets, or sides, with three meeting at each vertex.
    a. Thing
    c. Undefined
    b. Cube0
    d. Undefined

125. A _____ is a three-dimensional geometric shape formed by straight lines through a fixed point (vertex) to the points of a fixed curve (directrix)
    a. Concept
    c. Undefined
    b. Cone0
    d. Undefined

126. In physics, _____ is an influence that may cause an object to accelerate. It may be experienced as a lift, a push, or a pull. The actual acceleration of the body is determined by the vector sum of all forces acting on it, known as net _____ or resultant _____.
    a. Thing
    c. Undefined
    b. Force0
    d. Undefined

127. _____ is a term applied when talking about the movement of air from one place to the next.
    a. Wind speed0
    c. Undefined
    b. Thing
    d. Undefined

128. A _____ is a movement of an object in a circular motion. A two-dimensional object rotates around a center (or point) of _____. A three-dimensional object rotates around a line called an axis. If the axis of _____ is within the body, the body is said to rotate upon itself, or spin—which implies relative speed and perhaps free-movement with angular momentum. A circular motion about an external point, e.g. the Earth about the Sun, is called an orbit or more properly an orbital revolution.
    a. Rotation0
    c. Undefined
    b. Thing
    d. Undefined

129. In physics, the _____ momentum of an object rotating about some reference point is the measure of the extent to which the object will continue to rotate about that point unless acted upon by an external torque.
    a. Thing
    c. Undefined
    b. Angular0
    d. Undefined

130. _____ is a scalar measure of rotation rate. It is the magnitude of the vector quantity angular velocity.
    a. Thing
    c. Undefined
    b. Angular frequency0
    d. Undefined

131. _____ is a scalar measure of rotation rate. It is the magnitude of the vector quantity angular velocity.
    a. Thing
    c. Undefined
    b. Angular speed0
    d. Undefined

132. A _____ is a set of numbers that designate location in a given reference system, such as x,y in a planar _____ system or an x,y,z in a three-dimensional _____ system.

Chapter 6. RATIONAL EXPRESSIONS

    a. Coordinate0
    c. Undefined
    b. Thing
    d. Undefined

133. In mathematics and its applications, a _____ is a system for assigning an n-tuple of numbers or scalars to each point in an n-dimensional space.
    a. Coordinate system0
    c. Undefined
    b. Concept
    d. Undefined

134. In Euclidean geometry, a _____ is the set of all points in a plane at a fixed distance, called the radius, from a given point, the center.
    a. Circle0
    c. Undefined
    b. Thing
    d. Undefined

135. A _____ is a unit of length in the metric system, equal to one thousand metres, the current SI base unit of length
    a. Thing
    c. Undefined
    b. Kilometer0
    d. Undefined

136. _____ is a synonym for information.
    a. Data0
    c. Undefined
    b. Thing
    d. Undefined

137. In mathematics, an _____, mean, or central tendency of a data set refers to a measure of the "middle" or "expected" value of the data set.
    a. Average0
    c. Undefined
    b. Concept
    d. Undefined

138. Deductive _____ is the kind of _____ in which the conclusion is necessitated by, or reached from, previously known facts (the premises).
    a. Thing
    c. Undefined
    b. Reasoning0
    d. Undefined

139. In business, particularly accounting, a _____ is the time intervals that the accounts, statement, payments, or other calculations cover.
    a. Thing
    c. Undefined
    b. Period0
    d. Undefined

140. _____ variables are variables other than the independent variable that may bear any effect on the behavior of the subject being studied.
    a. Extraneous0
    c. Undefined
    b. Thing
    d. Undefined

141. _____ is the application of tools and a processing medium to the transformation of raw materials into finished goods for sale.
    a. Manufacturing0
    c. Undefined
    b. Thing
    d. Undefined

Chapter 6. RATIONAL EXPRESSIONS 83

142. In mathematics, a _____ is the set of all points in three-dimensional space (R^3) which are at distance r from a fixed point of that space, where r is a positive real number called the radius of the _____. The fixed point is called the center or centre, and is not part of the _____ itself.
   a. Thing
   b. Sphere0
   c. Undefined
   d. Undefined

143. Any point where a graph makes contact with an coordinate axis is called an _____ of the graph
   a. Thing
   b. Intercept0
   c. Undefined
   d. Undefined

144. The Gaussian _____ is an algorithm which can be used to determine the solutions of a system of linear equations, to find the rank of a matrix, and to calculate the inverse of an invertible square matrix.
   a. Elimination method0
   b. Thing
   c. Undefined
   d. Undefined

145. A _____ is a function that assigns a number to subsets of a given set.
   a. Measure0
   b. Thing
   c. Undefined
   d. Undefined

146. In mathematics, a _____ is a rectangular table of numbers or, more generally, a table consisting of abstract quantities that can be added and multiplied.
   a. Matrix0
   b. Thing
   c. Undefined
   d. Undefined

147. A _____ is an individual or household that purchases and uses goods and services generated within the economy.
   a. Consumer0
   b. Thing
   c. Undefined
   d. Undefined

148. _____ are activities that are governed by a set of rules or customs and often engaged in competitively.
   a. Sports0
   b. Thing
   c. Undefined
   d. Undefined

149. _____ are the basic objects of study in graph theory. Informally speaking, a graph is a set of objects called points, nodes, or vertices connected by links called lines or edges.
   a. Thing
   b. Graphs0
   c. Undefined
   d. Undefined

Chapter 7. RATIONAL EXPONENTS, RADICALS, AND COMPLEX NUMBERS

1. In mathematics, a _____ number is a number which can be expressed as a ratio of two integers. Non-integer _____ numbers (commonly called fractions) are usually written as the vulgar fraction a / b, where b is not zero.
   a. Rational0
   b. Thing
   c. Undefined
   d. Undefined

2. _____ is a mathematical operation, written a^n, involving two numbers, the base a and the exponent n.
   a. Thing
   b. Exponentiating0
   c. Undefined
   d. Undefined

3. _____ is a mathematical operation, written a^n, involving two numbers, the base a and the exponent n.
   a. Exponentiation0
   b. Thing
   c. Undefined
   d. Undefined

4. In plane geometry, a _____ is a polygon with four equal sides, four right angles, and parallel opposite sides. In algebra, the _____ of a number is that number multiplied by itself.
   a. Thing
   b. Square0
   c. Undefined
   d. Undefined

5. In mathematics, a _____ of a number x is a number r such that $r^2 = x$, or in words, a number r whose square (the result of multiplying the number by itself) is x.
   a. Thing
   b. Square root0
   c. Undefined
   d. Undefined

6. In mathematics, a _____ of a complex-valued function f is a member x of the domain of f such that f(x) vanishes at x, that is, x : f (x) = 0.
   a. Thing
   b. Root0
   c. Undefined
   d. Undefined

7. _____ is the symbold used to indicate the nth root of a number
   a. Thing
   b. Radical0
   c. Undefined
   d. Undefined

8. An _____ is a combination of numbers, operators, grouping symbols and/or free variables and bound variables arranged in a meaningful way which can be evaluated..
   a. Thing
   b. Expression0
   c. Undefined
   d. Undefined

9. The _____ is the number or expression underneath the radical sign.
   a. Thing
   b. Radicand0
   c. Undefined
   d. Undefined

10. The _____ integers are all the integers from zero on upwards.
    a. Nonnegative0
    b. Thing
    c. Undefined
    d. Undefined

11. A _____ is a symbolic representation denoting a quantity or expression. It often represents an "unknown" quantity that has the potential to change.

Chapter 7. RATIONAL EXPONENTS, RADICALS, AND COMPLEX NUMBERS

a. Variable0
b. Thing
c. Undefined
d. Undefined

12. In mathematics, _____ are used to indicate the square root of a number.
a. Thing
b. Radicals0
c. Undefined
d. Undefined

13. The mathematical concept of a _____ expresses the intuitive idea of deterministic dependence between two quantities, one of which is viewed as primary and the other as secondary. A _____ then is a way to associate a unique output for each input of a specified type, for example, a real number or an element of a given set.
a. Function0
b. Thing
c. Undefined
d. Undefined

14. In mathematics, a _____ may be described informally as a number that can be given by an infinite decimal representation.
a. Real number0
b. Thing
c. Undefined
d. Undefined

15. A _____ is a number that is less than zero.
a. Negative number0
b. Thing
c. Undefined
d. Undefined

16. The term _____ can refer to an integer which is the square of some other integer, or an algebraic expression that can be factored as the square of some other expression.
a. Perfect square0
b. Thing
c. Undefined
d. Undefined

17. In mathematics, an _____ number is any real number that is not a rational number- that is, it is a number which cannot be expressed as a fraction m/n, where m and n are integers.
a. Thing
b. Irrational0
c. Undefined
d. Undefined

18. In mathematics, an _____ is any real number that is not a rational number ¡ª that is, it is a number which cannot be expressed as m/n, where m and n are integers.
a. Irrational number0
b. Thing
c. Undefined
d. Undefined

19. A _____ is a negotiable instrument instructing a financial institution to pay a specific amount of a specific currency from a specific demand account held in the maker/depositor's name with that institution. Both the maker and payee may be natural persons or legal entities.
a. Thing
b. Check0
c. Undefined
d. Undefined

20. A _____ is a three-dimensional solid object bounded by six square faces, facets, or sides, with three meeting at each vertex.

Chapter 7. RATIONAL EXPONENTS, RADICALS, AND COMPLEX NUMBERS

a. Cube0
b. Thing
c. Undefined
d. Undefined

21. A _____ of a number is a number a such that $a^3 = x$.
    a. Thing
    b. Cube root0
    c. Undefined
    d. Undefined

22. _____ has many meanings, most of which simply .
    a. Power0
    b. Thing
    c. Undefined
    d. Undefined

23. An _____ of a number a is a number b such that $b^n = a$.
    a. Thing
    b. Nth root0
    c. Undefined
    d. Undefined

24. _____ are objects, characters, or other concrete representations of ideas, concepts, or other abstractions.
    a. Symbols0
    b. Thing
    c. Undefined
    d. Undefined

25. The word _____ is used in a variety of ways in mathematics.
    a. Index0
    b. Thing
    c. Undefined
    d. Undefined

26. In mathematics, the additive inverse, or _____ of a number n is the number that, when added to n, yields zero. The additive inverse of n is denoted −n. For example, 7 is −7, because 7 + (−7) = 0, and the additive inverse of −0.3 is 0.3, because −0.3 + 0.3 = 0.
    a. Thing
    b. Opposite0
    c. Undefined
    d. Undefined

27. In mathematics, the _____ of a number n is the number that, when added to n, yields zero. The _____ of n is denoted −n. For example, 7 is −7, because 7 + (−7) = 0, and the _____ of −0.3 is 0.3, because −0.3 + 0.3 = 0.
    a. Additive inverse0
    b. Thing
    c. Undefined
    d. Undefined

28. Mathematical _____ is used to represent ideas.
    a. Notation0
    b. Thing
    c. Undefined
    d. Undefined

29. The _____ (symbol _____) and the millibar (symbol mbar, also mb) are units of pressure.
    a. Thing
    b. Bar0
    c. Undefined
    d. Undefined

30. In mathematics, the _____ (or modulus) of a real number is its numerical value without regard to its sign.
    a. Thing
    b. Absolute value0
    c. Undefined
    d. Undefined

Chapter 7. RATIONAL EXPONENTS, RADICALS, AND COMPLEX NUMBERS

31. _____ is a test to determine if a relation or its graph is a function or not
    a. Thing
    b. Vertical line test0
    c. Undefined
    d. Undefined

32. Acid _____ ratio measures the ability of a company to use its near cash or quick assets to immediately extinguish its current liabilities.
    a. Thing
    b. Test0
    c. Undefined
    d. Undefined

33. In mathematics, a _____ of a k-place relation $L \subseteq X_1 \times ... \times X_k$ is one of the sets X_j, $1 \leq j \leq k$. In the special case where k = 2 and $L \subseteq X_1 \times X_2$ is a function $L : X_1 \to X_2$, it is conventional to refer to X_1 as the _____ of the function and to refer to X_2 as the codomain of the function.
    a. Domain0
    b. Thing
    c. Undefined
    d. Undefined

34. In mathematics, the concept of a _____ tries to capture the intuitive idea of a geometrical one-dimensional and continuous object. A simple example is the circle.
    a. Curve0
    b. Thing
    c. Undefined
    d. Undefined

35. _____ of an object is its speed in a particular direction.
    a. Thing
    b. Velocity0
    c. Undefined
    d. Undefined

36. In mathematics, an inequality is a statement about the relative size or order of two objects. For example 14 > 10, or 14 is _____ 10.
    a. Thing
    b. Greater than0
    c. Undefined
    d. Undefined

37. For a given gravitational field and a given position, the _____ is the minimum speed an object without propulsion needs to have to move away indefinitely from the source of the field, as opposed to falling back or staying in an orbit within a bounded distance from the source.
    a. Thing
    b. Escape velocity0
    c. Undefined
    d. Undefined

38. A _____, as defined by the International Astronomical Union, is a celestial body orbiting a star or stellar remnant that is massive enough to be rounded by its own gravity, not massive enough to cause thermonuclear fusion in its core, and has cleared its neighboring region of planetesimals.
    a. Planet0
    b. Thing
    c. Undefined
    d. Undefined

39. _____ algebra (sometimes called General algebra) is the field of mathematics that studies the ideas common to all algebraic structures.
    a. Thing
    b. Universal0
    c. Undefined
    d. Undefined

Chapter 7. RATIONAL EXPONENTS, RADICALS, AND COMPLEX NUMBERS

40. In classical geometry, a _____ of a circle or sphere is any line segment from its center to its boundary. By extension, the _____ of a circle or sphere is the length of any such segment. The _____ is half the diameter. In science and engineering the term _____ of curvature is commonly used as a synonym for _____.
   a. Thing
   b. Radius0
   c. Undefined
   d. Undefined

41. _____ is the property of a physical object that quantifies the amount of matter and energy it is equivalent to.
   a. Mass0
   b. Thing
   c. Undefined
   d. Undefined

42. In mathematics and the mathematical sciences, a _____ is a fixed, but possibly unspecified, value. This is in contrast to a variable, which is not fixed.
   a. Thing
   b. Constant0
   c. Undefined
   d. Undefined

43. In geometry, the _____ of an object is a point in some sense in the middle of the object.
   a. Center0
   b. Thing
   c. Undefined
   d. Undefined

44. _____ is a set, with some particular properties and usually some additional structure, such as the operations of addition or multiplication, for instance.
   a. Space0
   b. Thing
   c. Undefined
   d. Undefined

45. _____ is a synonym for information.
   a. Thing
   b. Data0
   c. Undefined
   d. Undefined

46. In mathematics, _____ growth occurs when the growth rate of a function is always proportional to the function's current size.
   a. Exponential0
   b. Thing
   c. Undefined
   d. Undefined

47. In mathematics, a _____ is the result of multiplying, or an expression that identifies factors to be multiplied.
   a. Thing
   b. Product0
   c. Undefined
   d. Undefined

48. The _____ governs the differentiation of products of differentiable functions.
   a. Product rule0
   b. Thing
   c. Undefined
   d. Undefined

49. A _____ is the part of a fraction that tells how many equal parts make up a whole, and which is used in the name of the fraction: "halves", "thirds", "fourths" or "quarters", "fifths" and so on.
   a. Denominator0
   b. Concept
   c. Undefined
   d. Undefined

Chapter 7. RATIONAL EXPONENTS, RADICALS, AND COMPLEX NUMBERS

50. In physics, the _____ momentum of an object rotating about some reference point is the measure of the extent to which the object will continue to rotate about that point unless acted upon by an external torque.
   a. Angular0
   b. Thing
   c. Undefined
   d. Undefined

51. _____ is a scalar measure of rotation rate. It is the magnitude of the vector quantity angular velocity.
   a. Angular frequency0
   b. Thing
   c. Undefined
   d. Undefined

52. In statistics the _____ of an event i is the number n_i of times the event occurred in the experiment or the study. These frequencies are often graphically represented in histograms.
   a. Concept
   b. Frequency0
   c. Undefined
   d. Undefined

53. A _____ is a special kind of ratio, indicating a relationship between two measurements with different units, such as miles to gallons or cents to pounds.
   a. Thing
   b. Rate0
   c. Undefined
   d. Undefined

54. The _____ or kilogramme is the SI base unit of mass. It is defined as being equal to the mass of the international prototype of the _____.
   a. Kilogram0
   b. Thing
   c. Undefined
   d. Undefined

55. In topology and related areas of mathematics a _____ or Moore-Smith sequence is a generalization of a sequence, intended to unify the various notions of limit and generalize them to arbitrary topological spaces.
   a. Net0
   b. Thing
   c. Undefined
   d. Undefined

56. _____ is a business term for the amount of money that a company receives from its activities in a given period, mostly from sales of products and/or services to customers
   a. Thing
   b. Revenue0
   c. Undefined
   d. Undefined

57. In mathematics, factorization (British English: factorisation) or factoring is the decomposition of an object (for example, a number, a polynomial, or a matrix) into a product of other objects, or _____, which when multiplied together give the original.
   a. Thing
   b. Factors0
   c. Undefined
   d. Undefined

58. The _____ are the only integral domain whose positive elements are well-ordered, and in which order is preserved by addition. Like the natural numbers, the _____ form a countably infinite set. The set of all _____ is usually denoted in mathematics by a boldface Z .
   a. Thing
   b. Integers0
   c. Undefined
   d. Undefined

Chapter 7. RATIONAL EXPONENTS, RADICALS, AND COMPLEX NUMBERS

59. A _____ is a number which is the cube of an integer.
    a. Thing
    b. Perfect cube0
    c. Undefined
    d. Undefined

60. In mathematics, _____ expressions is used to reduce the expression into the lowest possible term.
    a. Thing
    b. Simplifying0
    c. Undefined
    d. Undefined

61. In mathematics, a _____ is the end result of a division problem. It can also be expressed as the number of times the divisor divides into the dividend.
    a. Quotient0
    b. Thing
    c. Undefined
    d. Undefined

62. The _____ is a method of finding the derivative of a function that is the quotient of two other functions for which derivatives exist.
    a. Thing
    b. Quotient rule0
    c. Undefined
    d. Undefined

63. The _____, the average in everyday English, which is also called the arithmetic _____ (and is distinguished from the geometric _____ or harmonic _____). The average is also called the sample _____. The expected value of a random variable, which is also called the population _____.
    a. Thing
    b. Mean0
    c. Undefined
    d. Undefined

64. A _____ is a three-dimensional geometric shape formed by straight lines through a fixed point (vertex) to the points of a fixed curve (directrix)
    a. Cone0
    b. Concept
    c. Undefined
    d. Undefined

65. In Graph theory, a _____ is a digraph with weighted edges.
    a. Concept
    b. Network0
    c. Undefined
    d. Undefined

66. In economics, supply and _____ describe market relations between prospective sellers and buyers of a good.
    a. Demand0
    b. Thing
    c. Undefined
    d. Undefined

67. A _____ is the result of the addition of a set of numbers. The numbers may be natural numbers, complex numbers, matrices, or still more complicated objects. An infinite _____ is a subtle procedure known as a series.
    a. Thing
    b. Sum0
    c. Undefined
    d. Undefined

68. In mathematics, and in particular in abstract algebra, the _____ is a property of binary operations that generalises the distributive law from elementary algebra.

Chapter 7. RATIONAL EXPONENTS, RADICALS, AND COMPLEX NUMBERS 91

   a. Distributive property0
   c. Undefined
   b. Thing
   d. Undefined

69. A _____ is a numeral used to indicate a count. The most common use of the word today is to name the part of a fraction that tells the number or count of equal parts.
   a. Numerator0
   c. Undefined
   b. Thing
   d. Undefined

70. _____ is the practice of doing mathematical calculations using only the human brain, with no help from any computing devices.
   a. Concept
   c. Undefined
   b. Mental math0
   d. Undefined

71. The metre (or _____, see spelling differences) is a measure of length. It is the basic unit of length in the metric system and in the International System of Units (SI), used around the world for general and scientific purposes.
   a. Concept
   c. Undefined
   b. Meter0
   d. Undefined

72. _____ is the distance around a given two-dimensional object. As a general rule, the _____ of a polygon can always be calculated by adding all the length of the sides together. So, the formula for triangles is P = a + b + c, where a, b and c stand for each side of it. For quadrilaterals the equation is P = a + b + c + d. For equilateral polygons, P = na, where n is the number of sides and a is the side length.
   a. Thing
   c. Undefined
   b. Perimeter0
   d. Undefined

73. _____, or Rationalisation in mathematics is the process of removing a square root or imaginary number from the denominator of a fraction.
   a. Rationalizing0
   c. Undefined
   b. Thing
   d. Undefined

74. Equivalence is the condition of being _____ or essentially equal.
   a. Thing
   c. Undefined
   b. Equivalent0
   d. Undefined

75. A _____ signifies a point or points of probability on a subject e.g., the _____ of creativity, which allows for the formation of rule or norm or law by interpretation of the phenomena events that can be created.
   a. Principle0
   c. Undefined
   b. Thing
   d. Undefined

76. In algebra, a _____ is a binomial formed by taking the opposite of the second term of a binomial.
   a. Conjugate0
   c. Undefined
   b. Thing
   d. Undefined

77. The _____ of a solid object is the three-dimensional concept of how much space it occupies, often quantified numerically.

Chapter 7. RATIONAL EXPONENTS, RADICALS, AND COMPLEX NUMBERS

    a. Thing
    b. Volume0
    c. Undefined
    d. Undefined

78. _____ forms part of thinking. Considered the most complex of all intellectual functions, _____ has been defined as higher-order cognitive process that requires the modulation and control of more routine or fundamental skills.
    a. Problem solving0
    b. Thing
    c. Undefined
    d. Undefined

79. _____ is a relation in Euclidean geometry among the three sides of a right triangle.
    a. Thing
    b. Pythagorean Theorem0
    c. Undefined
    d. Undefined

80. In mathematics, a _____ is a statement that can be proved on the basis of explicitly stated or previously agreed assumptions.
    a. Theorem0
    b. Thing
    c. Undefined
    d. Undefined

81. _____ is a method for differentiating expressions involving exponentiation the power operation.
    a. Power rule0
    b. Thing
    c. Undefined
    d. Undefined

82. _____ variables are variables other than the independent variable that may bear any effect on the behavior of the subject being studied.
    a. Extraneous0
    b. Thing
    c. Undefined
    d. Undefined

83. In mathematics, a _____ is a polynomial equation of the second degree. The general form is $ax^2 + bx + c = 0$.
    a. Quadratic equation0
    b. Thing
    c. Undefined
    d. Undefined

84. In mathematics, _____ is the decomposition of an object into a product of other objects, or factors, which when multiplied together give the original.
    a. Factoring0
    b. Thing
    c. Undefined
    d. Undefined

85. In elementary algebra, a _____ is a polynomial with two terms: the sum of two monomials. It is the simplest kind of polynomial except for a monomial.
    a. Thing
    b. Binomial0
    c. Undefined
    d. Undefined

86. A _____ is one of the basic shapes of geometry: a polygon with three vertices and three sides which are straight line segments.
    a. Thing
    b. Triangle0
    c. Undefined
    d. Undefined

Chapter 7. RATIONAL EXPONENTS, RADICALS, AND COMPLEX NUMBERS

87. In a right triangle, the _____ of the triangle are the two sides that are perpendicular to each other, as opposed to the hypotenuse.
    a. Thing
    b. Legs0
    c. Undefined
    d. Undefined

88. The _____ of a right triangle is the triangle's longest side; the side opposite the right angle.
    a. Thing
    b. Hypotenuse0
    c. Undefined
    d. Undefined

89. _____ has one 90° internal angle a right angle.
    a. Right triangle0
    b. Thing
    c. Undefined
    d. Undefined

90. In mathematics, the _____ of two sets A and B is the set that contains all elements of A that also belong to B (or equivalently, all elements of B that also belong to A), but no other elements.
    a. Intersection0
    b. Thing
    c. Undefined
    d. Undefined

91. In linear algebra, the _____ of an n-by-n square matrix A is defined to be the sum of the elements on the main diagonal of A,
    a. Thing
    b. Trace0
    c. Undefined
    d. Undefined

92. In geographic information systems, a _____ comprises an entity with a geographic location, typically determined by points, arcs, or polygons. Carriageways and cadastres exemplify _____ data.
    a. Feature0
    b. Thing
    c. Undefined
    d. Undefined

93. In abstract algebra, _____ consists of sets with binary operations that satisfy certain axioms.
    a. Grouping0
    b. Thing
    c. Undefined
    d. Undefined

94. A _____ decimal is a number whose decimal representation eventually becomes periodic (i.e. the same number sequence _____ indefinitely).
    a. Repeating0
    b. Thing
    c. Undefined
    d. Undefined

95. _____ is a state in both the Midwestern and Western regions of the United States of America. It is the northernmost of the Great Plains states and is the northern half of The Dakotas.
    a. Thing
    b. North Dakota0
    c. Undefined
    d. Undefined

96. In mathematics, a _____ is the set of all points in three-dimensional space (R^3) which are at distance r from a fixed point of that space, where r is a positive real number called the radius of the _____. The fixed point is called the center or centre, and is not part of the _____ itself.

Chapter 7. RATIONAL EXPONENTS, RADICALS, AND COMPLEX NUMBERS

a. Thing
b. Sphere0
c. Undefined
d. Undefined

97. A _____ is a unit of length, usually used to measure distance, in a number of different systems, including Imperial units, United States customary units and Norwegian/Swedish mil. Its size can vary from system to system, but in each is between 1 and 10 kilometers. In contemporary English contexts _____ refers to either:
a. Thing
b. Mile0
c. Undefined
d. Undefined

98. _____ is a unit of speed, expressing the number of international miles covered per hour.
a. Thing
b. Miles per hour0
c. Undefined
d. Undefined

99. In geometry and trigonometry, a _____ is defined as an angle between two straight intersecting lines of ninety degrees, or one-quarter of a circle.
a. Right angle0
b. Thing
c. Undefined
d. Undefined

100. In physics, _____ is an influence that may cause an object to accelerate. It may be experienced as a lift, a push, or a pull. The actual acceleration of the body is determined by the vector sum of all forces acting on it, known as net _____ or resultant _____.
a. Force0
b. Thing
c. Undefined
d. Undefined

101. A _____ is a unit of length in the metric system, equal to one thousand metres, the current SI base unit of length
a. Kilometer0
b. Thing
c. Undefined
d. Undefined

102. In business, _____, _____ cost or _____ expense refers to an ongoing expense of operating a business.
a. Overhead0
b. Thing
c. Undefined
d. Undefined

103. In mathematics, the _____ f is the collection of all ordered pairs . In particular, graph means the graphical representation of this collection, in the form of a curve or surface, together with axes, etc. Graphing on a Cartesian plane is sometimes referred to as curve sketching.
a. Thing
b. Graph of a function0
c. Undefined
d. Undefined

104. In mathematics, a _____ is a number in the form of a + bi where a and b are real numbers, and i is the imaginary unit, with the property i 2 = −1. The real number a is called the real part of the _____, and the real number b is the imaginary part.
a. Thing
b. Complex number0
c. Undefined
d. Undefined

Chapter 7. RATIONAL EXPONENTS, RADICALS, AND COMPLEX NUMBERS

105. In mathematics, an _____ number is a complex number whose square is a negative real number. They were defined in 1572 by Rafael Bombelli.
   a. Imaginary0
   b. Thing
   c. Undefined
   d. Undefined

106. _____ is a set of numbers, in the broadest sense of the word, together with one or more operations, such as addition or multiplication.
   a. Thing
   b. Number system0
   c. Undefined
   d. Undefined

107. In mathematics, the _____ i (or sometimes the Latin j or the Greek iota, see below) allows the real number system R to be extended to the complex number system C. Its precise definition is dependent upon the particular method of extension.
   a. Thing
   b. Imaginary unit0
   c. Undefined
   d. Undefined

108. A _____ is a set whose members are members of another set or a set contained within another set.
   a. Subset0
   b. Thing
   c. Undefined
   d. Undefined

109. In mathematics, an _____ is a complex number whose square is a negative real number. They were defined in 1572 by Rafael Bombelli.
   a. Imaginary number0
   b. Thing
   c. Undefined
   d. Undefined

110. In mathematics, _____ are any real number that is not a rational number ¡ª that is, it is a number which cannot be expressed as m/n, where m and n are integers.
   a. Thing
   b. Irrational numbers0
   c. Undefined
   d. Undefined

111. In mathematics, the _____ of a complex number z, is the first element of the ordered pair of real numbers representing z, i.e. if z = (x,y), or equivalently, z = x + iy, then the _____ of z is x. It is denoted by Re{z} . The complex function which maps z to the _____ of z is not holomorphic.
   a. Thing
   b. Real part0
   c. Undefined
   d. Undefined

112. In mathematics, the _____ of a complex number z, is the second element of the ordered pair of real numbers representing z, i.e. if z = (x,y), or equivalently, z = x + iy, then the _____ of z is y.
   a. Imaginary part0
   b. Thing
   c. Undefined
   d. Undefined

113. _____ also sometimes known as the double distributive property or more colloquially as foiling, is commonly taught to US high school students learning algebra as a mnemonic for remembering how to multiply two binomials polynomials with two terms.

Chapter 7. RATIONAL EXPONENTS, RADICALS, AND COMPLEX NUMBERS

a. Thing
b. FOIL method0
c. Undefined
d. Undefined

114. The _____ is commonly taught to US high school students learning algebra as a mnemonic for remembering how to multiply two binomials.
a. FOIL rule0
b. Thing
c. Undefined
d. Undefined

115. In mathematics, _____ is an elementary arithmetic operation. When one of the numbers is a whole number, _____ is the repeated sum of the other number.
a. Thing
b. Multiplication0
c. Undefined
d. Undefined

116. A _____ is a function that assigns a number to subsets of a given set.
a. Thing
b. Measure0
c. Undefined
d. Undefined

117. _____ is the transport of people on a trip/journey or the process or time involved in a person or object moving from one location to another.
a. Thing
b. Travel0
c. Undefined
d. Undefined

118. A _____ is an object that is attached to a pivot point so that it can swing freely.
a. Pendulum0
b. Thing
c. Undefined
d. Undefined

119. In business, particularly accounting, a _____ is the time intervals that the accounts, statement, payments, or other calculations cover.
a. Period0
b. Thing
c. Undefined
d. Undefined

120. In mathematics, an _____, mean, or central tendency of a data set refers to a measure of the "middle" or "expected" value of the data set.
a. Concept
b. Average0
c. Undefined
d. Undefined

121. In mathematics, a matrix can be thought of as each row or _____ being a vector. Hence, a space formed by row vectors or _____ vectors are said to be a row space or a _____ space.
a. Concept
b. Column0
c. Undefined
d. Undefined

122. In mathematics, the word _____ is used informally to refer to certain distinct bodies of knowledge about mathematics.
a. Thing
b. Theoretical0
c. Undefined
d. Undefined

Chapter 7. RATIONAL EXPONENTS, RADICALS, AND COMPLEX NUMBERS

123. In Euclidean geometry, a _____ is the set of all points in a plane at a fixed distance, called the radius, from a given point, the center.
    a. Thing
    b. Circle0
    c. Undefined
    d. Undefined

124. In mathematics, _____ refers to a number of loosely related concepts in different areas of geometry. Intuitively, _____ is the amount by which a geometric object deviates from being flat, but this is defined in different ways depending on the context
    a. Thing
    b. Curvature0
    c. Undefined
    d. Undefined

125. In mathematics, a _____ can mean either an element of the set {1, 2, 3, ...} (i.e the positive integers) or an element of the set {0, 1, 2, 3, ...} (i.e. the non-negative integers).
    a. Concept
    b. Whole number0
    c. Undefined
    d. Undefined

126. The payment of _____ as remuneration for services rendered or products sold is a common way to reward sales people.
    a. Commission0
    b. Thing
    c. Undefined
    d. Undefined

127. In mathematics, the _____ of a function is the set of all "output" values produced by that function. Given a function $f : A \to B$, the _____ of f, is defined to be the set $\{x \in B : x = f(a) \text{ for some } a \in A\}$.
    a. Thing
    b. Range0
    c. Undefined
    d. Undefined

128. _____ is often used to describe the measurement of the steepness, incline, gradient, or grade of a straight line. The _____ is defined as the ratio of the "rise" divided by the "run" between two points on a line, or in other words, the ratio of the altitude change to the horizontal distance between any two points on the line.
    a. Thing
    b. Slope0
    c. Undefined
    d. Undefined

129. The _____ is used to discard one of the variables in an equation, only to replace it with the actual value when solving multiple equations.
    a. Substitution method0
    b. Thing
    c. Undefined
    d. Undefined

130. _____ element of an element x with respect to a binary operation * with identity element e is an element y such that x * y = y * x = e. In particular,
    a. Inverse0
    b. Thing
    c. Undefined
    d. Undefined

Chapter 8. QUADRATIC EQUATIONS AND FUNCTIONS

1. _____ is the level of functional and/or metabolic efficiency of an organism at both the micro level.
   a. Thing
   b. Health0
   c. Undefined
   d. Undefined

2. _____ is the fee paid on borrowed money.
   a. Interest0
   b. Thing
   c. Undefined
   d. Undefined

3. In geometry, the _____ of an object is a point in some sense in the middle of the object.
   a. Center0
   b. Thing
   c. Undefined
   d. Undefined

4. In mathematics, a _____ is the result of multiplying, or an expression that identifies factors to be multiplied.
   a. Thing
   b. Product0
   c. Undefined
   d. Undefined

5. _____ the expected value of a random variable displays the average or central value of the variable. It is a summary value of the distribution of the variable.
   a. Thing
   b. Determining0
   c. Undefined
   d. Undefined

6. _____ is a branch of mathematics concerning the study of structure, relation and quantity.
   a. Algebra0
   b. Concept
   c. Undefined
   d. Undefined

7. In mathematics, a _____ is a polynomial equation of the second degree. The general form is $ax^2 + bx + c = 0$.
   a. Quadratic equation0
   b. Thing
   c. Undefined
   d. Undefined

8. In mathematics, a _____ is an expression that is constructed from one or more variables and constants, using only the operations of addition, subtraction, multiplication, and constant positive whole number exponents. is a _____. Note in particular that division by an expression containing a variable is not in general allowed in polynomials. [1]
   a. Thing
   b. Polynomial0
   c. Undefined
   d. Undefined

9. The mathematical concept of a _____ expresses the intuitive idea of deterministic dependence between two quantities, one of which is viewed as primary and the other as secondary. A _____ then is a way to associate a unique output for each input of a specified type, for example, a real number or an element of a given set.
   a. Thing
   b. Function0
   c. Undefined
   d. Undefined

10. A _____ is a symbolic representation denoting a quantity or expression. It often represents an "unknown" quantity that has the potential to change.
    a. Variable0
    b. Thing
    c. Undefined
    d. Undefined

Chapter 8. QUADRATIC EQUATIONS AND FUNCTIONS

11. _____ systems represent systems whose behavior is not expressible as a sum of the behaviors of its descriptors.
    a. Thing
    b. Nonlinear0
    c. Undefined
    d. Undefined

12. In mathematics, an _____ is a statement about the relative size or order of two objects.
    a. Thing
    b. Inequality0
    c. Undefined
    d. Undefined

13. In mathematics, _____ is the decomposition of an object into a product of other objects, or factors, which when multiplied together give the original.
    a. Factoring0
    b. Thing
    c. Undefined
    d. Undefined

14. In mathematics, a _____ may be described informally as a number that can be given by an infinite decimal representation.
    a. Thing
    b. Real number0
    c. Undefined
    d. Undefined

15. In mathematics, a _____ is a statement that can be proved on the basis of explicitly stated or previously agreed assumptions.
    a. Thing
    b. Theorem0
    c. Undefined
    d. Undefined

16. _____ is a notation for writing numbers that is often used by scientists and mathematicians to make it easier to write large and small numbers.
    a. Scientific notation0
    b. Thing
    c. Undefined
    d. Undefined

17. A _____ is a set of possible values that a variable can take on in order to satisfy a given set of conditions, which may include equations and inequalities.
    a. Thing
    b. Solution set0
    c. Undefined
    d. Undefined

18. In plane geometry, a _____ is a polygon with four equal sides, four right angles, and parallel opposite sides. In algebra, the _____ of a number is that number multiplied by itself.
    a. Square0
    b. Thing
    c. Undefined
    d. Undefined

19. In mathematics, a _____ of a number x is a number r such that $r^2 = x$, or in words, a number r whose square (the result of multiplying the number by itself) is x.
    a. Thing
    b. Square root0
    c. Undefined
    d. Undefined

20. In mathematics, a _____ of a complex-valued function f is a member x of the domain of f such that f(x) vanishes at x, that is, x : f (x) = 0.

Chapter 8. QUADRATIC EQUATIONS AND FUNCTIONS

    a. Thing
    b. Root0
    c. Undefined
    d. Undefined

21. Mathematical _____ is used to represent ideas.
    a. Notation0
    b. Thing
    c. Undefined
    d. Undefined

22. _____ is a technique used in algebra to solve quadratic equations, in analytic geometry for determining the shapes of graphs, and in calculus for computing integrals, including, but hardly limited to, the integrals that define Laplace transforms. The essential objective is to reduce a quadratic polynomial in a variable in an equation or expression to a squared polynomial of linear order. This can reduce an equation or integral to one that is more easily solved or evaluated.
    a. Completing the square0
    b. Thing
    c. Undefined
    d. Undefined

23. A _____ is a negotiable instrument instructing a financial institution to pay a specific amount of a specific currency from a specific demand account held in the maker/depositor's name with that institution. Both the maker and payee may be natural persons or legal entities.
    a. Thing
    b. Check0
    c. Undefined
    d. Undefined

24. _____ is the symbold used to indicate the nth root of a number
    a. Radical0
    b. Thing
    c. Undefined
    d. Undefined

25. A _____ is a polynomial consisting of three terms; in other words, it is the sum of three monomials.
    a. Trinomial0
    b. Thing
    c. Undefined
    d. Undefined

26. The term _____ can refer to an integer which is the square of some other integer, or an algebraic expression that can be factored as the square of some other expression.
    a. Perfect square0
    b. Thing
    c. Undefined
    d. Undefined

27. In elementary algebra, a _____ is a polynomial with two terms: the sum of two monomials. It is the simplest kind of polynomial except for a monomial.
    a. Thing
    b. Binomial0
    c. Undefined
    d. Undefined

28. In mathematics, factorization (British English: factorisation) or factoring is the decomposition of an object (for example, a number, a polynomial, or a matrix) into a product of other objects, or _____, which when multiplied together give the original.
    a. Thing
    b. Factors0
    c. Undefined
    d. Undefined

29. In mathematics, a _____ is a constant multiplicative factor of a certain object. The object can be such things as a variable, a vector, a function, etc. For example, the _____ of $9x^2$ is 9.

Chapter 8. QUADRATIC EQUATIONS AND FUNCTIONS

a. Thing
b. Coefficient0
c. Undefined
d. Undefined

30. In mathematics and the mathematical sciences, a _____ is a fixed, but possibly unspecified, value. This is in contrast to a variable, which is not fixed.
a. Constant0
b. Thing
c. Undefined
d. Undefined

31. _____ is a fixed, but possibly unspecified, value. This is in contrast to a variable, which is not fixed.
a. Thing
b. Constant term0
c. Undefined
d. Undefined

32. A _____ is a special kind of ratio, indicating a relationship between two measurements with different units, such as miles to gallons or cents to pounds.
a. Rate0
b. Thing
c. Undefined
d. Undefined

33. _____ interest refers to the fact that whenever interest is calculated, it is based not only on the original principal, but also on any unpaid interest that has been added to the principal.
a. Thing
b. Compound0
c. Undefined
d. Undefined

34. _____ refers to the fact that whenever interest is calculated, it is based not only on the original principal, but also on any unpaid interest that has been added to the principal. The more frequently interest is compounded, the faster the balance grows.
a. Compound interest0
b. Concept
c. Undefined
d. Undefined

35. An _____ is the fee paid on borrow money.
a. Interest rate0
b. Concept
c. Undefined
d. Undefined

36. _____ is a kind of property which exists as magnitude or multitude. It is among the basic classes of things along with quality, substance, change, and relation.
a. Thing
b. Amount0
c. Undefined
d. Undefined

37. In business, particularly accounting, a _____ is the time intervals that the accounts, statement, payments, or other calculations cover.
a. Thing
b. Period0
c. Undefined
d. Undefined

38. _____ or investing is a term with several closely-related meanings in business management, finance and economics, related to saving or deferring consumption.

Chapter 8. QUADRATIC EQUATIONS AND FUNCTIONS

a. Investment0
b. Thing
c. Undefined
d. Undefined

39. The State of _____ is a state located in the Rocky Mountain region of the United States of America.
a. Thing
b. Colorado0
c. Undefined
d. Undefined

40. The payment of _____ as remuneration for services rendered or products sold is a common way to reward sales people.
a. Thing
b. Commission0
c. Undefined
d. Undefined

41. In Euclidean geometry, a _____ is the set of all points in a plane at a fixed distance, called the radius, from a given point, the center.
a. Thing
b. Circle0
c. Undefined
d. Undefined

42. A _____ is one of the basic shapes of geometry: a polygon with three vertices and three sides which are straight line segments.
a. Thing
b. Triangle0
c. Undefined
d. Undefined

43. In a right triangle, the _____ of the triangle are the two sides that are perpendicular to each other, as opposed to the hypotenuse.
a. Legs0
b. Thing
c. Undefined
d. Undefined

44. _____ has one 90° internal angle a right angle.
a. Right triangle0
b. Thing
c. Undefined
d. Undefined

45. An _____ triange is a triangle with at least two sides of equal length.
a. Isosceles0
b. Thing
c. Undefined
d. Undefined

46. The _____ of a right triangle is the triangle's longest side; the side opposite the right angle.
a. Hypotenuse0
b. Thing
c. Undefined
d. Undefined

47. A _____ is a function that assigns a number to subsets of a given set.
a. Measure0
b. Thing
c. Undefined
d. Undefined

48. A _____ can refer to a line joining two nonadjacent vertices of a polygon or polyhedron, or in some contexts any upward or downward sloping line. .

Chapter 8. QUADRATIC EQUATIONS AND FUNCTIONS

a. Diagonal0
b. Thing
c. Undefined
d. Undefined

49. In economics, supply and _____ describe market relations between prospective sellers and buyers of a good.
a. Thing
b. Demand0
c. Undefined
d. Undefined

50. An _____ is a combination of numbers, operators, grouping symbols and/or free variables and bound variables arranged in a meaningful way which can be evaluated..
a. Expression0
b. Thing
c. Undefined
d. Undefined

51. _____ is the application of tools and a processing medium to the transformation of raw materials into finished goods for sale.
a. Thing
b. Manufacturing0
c. Undefined
d. Undefined

52. A quadratic equation with real solutions, called roots, which may be real or complex, is given by the _____: $x = \frac{-b \pm \sqrt{b^2 - 4ac}}{2a}$.
a. Thing
b. Quadratic formula0
c. Undefined
d. Undefined

53. In mathematics, a _____ is an ordered list of objects. Like a set, it contains members, also called elements or terms, and the number of terms is called the length of the _____. Unlike a set, order matters, and the exact same elements can appear multiple times at different positions in the _____.
a. Thing
b. Sequence0
c. Undefined
d. Undefined

54. In mathematics, _____ expressions is used to reduce the expression into the lowest possible term.
a. Thing
b. Simplifying0
c. Undefined
d. Undefined

55. A _____ is a numeral used to indicate a count. The most common use of the word today is to name the part of a fraction that tells the number or count of equal parts.
a. Numerator0
b. Thing
c. Undefined
d. Undefined

56. Equivalence is the condition of being _____ or essentially equal.
a. Thing
b. Equivalent0
c. Undefined
d. Undefined

57. _____ of a polynomial with real or complex coefficients is a certain expression in the coefficients of the polynomial which is equal to zero if and only if the polynomial has a multiple root i.e. a root with multiplicity greater than one in the complex numbers.

Chapter 8. QUADRATIC EQUATIONS AND FUNCTIONS

a. Thing
b. Discriminant0
c. Undefined
d. Undefined

58. _____ is a relation in Euclidean geometry among the three sides of a right triangle.
a. Pythagorean Theorem0
b. Thing
c. Undefined
d. Undefined

59. In geometry and trigonometry, a _____ is defined as an angle between two straight intersecting lines of ninety degrees, or one-quarter of a circle.
a. Thing
b. Right angle0
c. Undefined
d. Undefined

60. A _____ is a deliberate process for transforming one or more inputs into one or more results.
a. Thing
b. Calculation0
c. Undefined
d. Undefined

61. An _____ is a term used to describe an allocation of money from one person to another.
a. Thing
b. Allowance0
c. Undefined
d. Undefined

62. In mathematics, an _____, mean, or central tendency of a data set refers to a measure of the "middle" or "expected" value of the data set.
a. Average0
b. Concept
c. Undefined
d. Undefined

63. A _____ is the result of the addition of a set of numbers. The numbers may be natural numbers, complex numbers, matrices, or still more complicated objects. An infinite _____ is a subtle procedure known as a series.
a. Sum0
b. Thing
c. Undefined
d. Undefined

64. The metre (or _____, see spelling differences) is a measure of length. It is the basic unit of length in the metric system and in the International System of Units (SI), used around the world for general and scientific purposes.
a. Concept
b. Meter0
c. Undefined
d. Undefined

65. In geometry, a _____ is defined as a quadrilateral where all four of its angles are right angles.
a. Thing
b. Rectangle0
c. Undefined
d. Undefined

66. _____ of an object is its speed in a particular direction.
a. Velocity0
b. Thing
c. Undefined
d. Undefined

67. Initial objects are also called _____, and terminal objects are also called final.

Chapter 8. QUADRATIC EQUATIONS AND FUNCTIONS   105

    a. Coterminal0
    b. Thing
    c. Undefined
    d. Undefined

68. _____ is a physical property of a system that underlies the common notions of hot and cold; something that is hotter has the greater _____.
    a. Temperature0
    b. Thing
    c. Undefined
    d. Undefined

69. A _____ is a polynomial function of the form $f(x) = ax^2 + bx + c$, where a, b, c are real numbers and a , 0.
    a. Quadratic function0
    b. Event
    c. Undefined
    d. Undefined

70. In mathematics, the _____ is a conic section generated by the intersection of a right circular conical surface and a plane parallel to a generating straight line of that surface. It can also be defined as locus of points in a plane which are equidistant from a given point.
    a. Thing
    b. Parabola0
    c. Undefined
    d. Undefined

71. _____ is a temperature scale named after the German physicist Daniel Gabriel _____ , who proposed it in 1724.
    a. Fahrenheit0
    b. Thing
    c. Undefined
    d. Undefined

72. In mathematics, there are several meanings of _____ depending on the subject.
    a. Degree0
    b. Thing
    c. Undefined
    d. Undefined

73. In topology and related areas of mathematics a _____ or Moore-Smith sequence is a generalization of a sequence, intended to unify the various notions of limit and generalize them to arbitrary topological spaces.
    a. Thing
    b. Net0
    c. Undefined
    d. Undefined

74. _____ is a synonym for information.
    a. Data0
    b. Thing
    c. Undefined
    d. Undefined

75. _____ is a mathematical science pertaining to the collection, analysis, interpretation or explanation, and presentation of data. It is applicable to a wide variety of academic disciplines, from the physical and social sciences to the humanities.
    a. Thing
    b. Statistics0
    c. Undefined
    d. Undefined

76. A _____ is the part of a fraction that tells how many equal parts make up a whole, and which is used in the name of the fraction: "halves", "thirds", "fourths" or "quarters", "fifths" and so on.

Chapter 8. QUADRATIC EQUATIONS AND FUNCTIONS

a. Denominator0
b. Concept
c. Undefined
d. Undefined

77. The _____, the average in everyday English, which is also called the arithmetic _____ (and is distinguished from the geometric _____ or harmonic _____). The average is also called the sample _____. The expected value of a random variable, which is also called the population _____.

a. Mean0
b. Thing
c. Undefined
d. Undefined

78. In mathematics, and in particular in abstract algebra, the _____ is a property of binary operations that generalises the distributive law from elementary algebra.

a. Thing
b. Distributive property0
c. Undefined
d. Undefined

79. _____ is the transport of people on a trip/journey or the process or time involved in a person or object moving from one location to another.

a. Thing
b. Travel0
c. Undefined
d. Undefined

80. In mathematics, a matrix can be thought of as each row or _____ being a vector. Hence, a space formed by row vectors or _____ vectors are said to be a row space or a _____ space.

a. Concept
b. Column0
c. Undefined
d. Undefined

81. A _____ is a unit of length, usually used to measure distance, in a number of different systems, including Imperial units, United States customary units and Norwegian/Swedish mil. Its size can vary from system to system, but in each is between 1 and 10 kilometers. In contemporary English contexts _____ refers to either:

a. Thing
b. Mile0
c. Undefined
d. Undefined

82. _____ is a unit of speed, expressing the number of international miles covered per hour.

a. Miles per hour0
b. Thing
c. Undefined
d. Undefined

83. _____ is a state located in the southern and southwestern regions of the United States of America.

a. Texas0
b. Thing
c. Undefined
d. Undefined

84. In mathematics, a _____ can mean either an element of the set {1, 2, 3, ...} (i.e the positive integers) or an element of the set {0, 1, 2, 3, ...} (i.e. the non-negative integers).

a. Whole number0
b. Concept
c. Undefined
d. Undefined

85. The _____ of a solid object is the three-dimensional concept of how much space it occupies, often quantified numerically.

Chapter 8. QUADRATIC EQUATIONS AND FUNCTIONS

    a. Volume0
    b. Thing
    c. Undefined
    d. Undefined

86. In mathematics, the _____ of a function is the set of all "output" values produced by that function. Given a function $f : A \to B$, the _____ of f, is defined to be the set $\{x \in B : x = f(a) \text{ for some } a \in A\}$.
    a. Range0
    b. Thing
    c. Undefined
    d. Undefined

87. In mathematics, a _____ of a k-place relation $L \subseteq X_1 \times \ldots \times X_k$ is one of the sets X_j, $1 \leq j \leq k$. In the special case where $k = 2$ and $L \subseteq X_1 \times X_2$ is a function $L : X_1 \to X_2$, it is conventional to refer to X_1 as the _____ of the function and to refer to X_2 as the codomain of the function.
    a. Thing
    b. Domain0
    c. Undefined
    d. Undefined

88. In mathematics, a _____ number is a number which can be expressed as a ratio of two integers. Non-integer _____ numbers (commonly called fractions) are usually written as the vulgar fraction a / b, where b is not zero.
    a. Thing
    b. Rational0
    c. Undefined
    d. Undefined

89. The word _____ comes from the Latin word linearis, which means created by lines.
    a. Linear0
    b. Thing
    c. Undefined
    d. Undefined

90. In common philosophical language, a proposition or _____, is the content of an assertion, that is, it is true-or-false and defined by the meaning of a particular piece of language.
    a. Concept
    b. Statement0
    c. Undefined
    d. Undefined

91. A _____ is a one-dimensional picture in which the integers are shown as specially-marked points evenly spaced on a line.
    a. Number line0
    b. Thing
    c. Undefined
    d. Undefined

92. Acid _____ ratio measures the ability of a company to use its near cash or quick assets to immediately extinguish its current liabilities.
    a. Test0
    b. Thing
    c. Undefined
    d. Undefined

93. In elementary algebra, an _____ is a set that contains every real number between two indicated numbers and may contain the two numbers themselves.
    a. Interval0
    b. Thing
    c. Undefined
    d. Undefined

94. _____ is the notation in which permitted values for a variable are expressed as ranging over a certain interval; "5 < x < 9" is an example of the application of _____.

Chapter 8. QUADRATIC EQUATIONS AND FUNCTIONS

a. Thing
b. Interval notation0
c. Undefined
d. Undefined

95. In mathematics, the multiplicative inverse of a number x, denoted 1/x or x^{-1}, is the number which, when multiplied by x, yields 1. The multiplicative inverse of x is also called the _____ of x.
a. Thing
b. Reciprocal0
c. Undefined
d. Undefined

96. The plus and _____ signs are mathematical symbols used to represent the notions of positive and negative as well as the operations of addition and subtraction.
a. Thing
b. Minus0
c. Undefined
d. Undefined

97. The _____ integers are all the integers from zero on upwards.
a. Thing
b. Nonnegative0
c. Undefined
d. Undefined

98. _____, from Latin meaning "to make progress", is defined in two different ways. Pure economic _____ is the increase in wealth that an investor has from making an investment, taking into consideration all costs associated with that investment including the opportunity cost of capital.
a. Profit0
b. Thing
c. Undefined
d. Undefined

99. The _____ of measurement are a globally standardized and modernized form of the metric system.
a. Units0
b. Thing
c. Undefined
d. Undefined

100. A _____ is any object propelled through space by the applicationp of a force.
a. Projectile0
b. Thing
c. Undefined
d. Undefined

101. In mathematics, an inequality is a statement about the relative size or order of two objects. For example 14 > 10, or 14 is _____ 10.
a. Greater than0
b. Thing
c. Undefined
d. Undefined

102. _____ are the basic objects of study in graph theory. Informally speaking, a graph is a set of objects called points, nodes, or vertices connected by links called lines or edges.
a. Thing
b. Graphs0
c. Undefined
d. Undefined

103. In geometry, a _____ is a special kind of point, usually a corner of a polygon, polyhedron, or higher dimensional polytope. In the geometry of curves a _____ is a point of where the first derivative of curvature is zero. In graph theory, a _____ is the fundamental unit out of which graphs are formed

Chapter 8. QUADRATIC EQUATIONS AND FUNCTIONS

a. Thing
b. Vertex0
c. Undefined
d. Undefined

104. _____ means "constancy", i.e. if something retains a certain feature even after we change a way of looking at it, then it is symmetric.
a. Thing
b. Symmetry0
c. Undefined
d. Undefined

105. An _____ is a straight line around which a geometric figure can be rotated.
a. Thing
b. Axis0
c. Undefined
d. Undefined

106. _____ of a two-dimensional figure is a line such that, if a perpendicular is constructed, any two points lying on the perpendicular at equal distances from the _____ are identical.
a. Axis of symmetry0
b. Thing
c. Undefined
d. Undefined

107. An _____ is when two lines intersect somewhere on a plane creating a right angle at intersection
a. Thing
b. Axes0
c. Undefined
d. Undefined

108. An _____ is a collection of two not necessarily distinct objects, one of which is distinguished as the first coordinate and the other as the second coordinate.
a. Thing
b. Ordered pair0
c. Undefined
d. Undefined

109. A _____ is a statement or claimt that a particular event will occur in the future in more certain terms than a forecast.
a. Prediction0
b. Thing
c. Undefined
d. Undefined

110. _____ is the practice of doing mathematical calculations using only the human brain, with no help from any computing devices.
a. Concept
b. Mental math0
c. Undefined
d. Undefined

111. A _____ fraction is a fraction in which the absolute value of the numerator is less than the denominator--hence, the absolute value of the fraction is less than 1.
a. Thing
b. Proper0
c. Undefined
d. Undefined

112. Any point where a graph makes contact with an coordinate axis is called an _____ of the graph
a. Intercept0
b. Thing
c. Undefined
d. Undefined

113. A _____ consists of one quarter of the coordinate plane.

Chapter 8. QUADRATIC EQUATIONS AND FUNCTIONS

    a. Quadrant0
    b. Thing
    c. Undefined
    d. Undefined

114. _____, either of the curved-bracket punctuation marks that together make a set of _____
    a. Parentheses0
    b. Thing
    c. Undefined
    d. Undefined

115. In mathematics a _____ is a function which defines a distance between elements of a set.
    a. Thing
    b. Metric0
    c. Undefined
    d. Undefined

116. In mathematics, the conjugate _____ or adjoint matrix of an m-by-n matrix A with complex entries is the n-by-m matrix A* obtained from A by taking the transpose and then taking the complex conjugate of each entry.
    a. Pairs0
    b. Thing
    c. Undefined
    d. Undefined

117. A _____ is an equation in which each term is either a constant or the product of a constant times the first power of a variable.
    a. Thing
    b. Linear equation0
    c. Undefined
    d. Undefined

118. In set theory and other branches of mathematics, the _____ of a collection of sets is the set that contains everything that belongs to any of the sets, but nothing else.
    a. Union0
    b. Thing
    c. Undefined
    d. Undefined

119. _____ is a way of expressing a number as a fraction of 100 per cent meaning "per hundred".
    a. Thing
    b. Percent0
    c. Undefined
    d. Undefined

120. A _____ is a number that is less than zero.
    a. Thing
    b. Negative number0
    c. Undefined
    d. Undefined

121. In mathematics, the _____ of a coordinate system is the point where the axes of the system intersect.
    a. Thing
    b. Origin0
    c. Undefined
    d. Undefined

122. _____ is often used to describe the measurement of the steepness, incline, gradient, or grade of a straight line. The _____ is defined as the ratio of the "rise" divided by the "run" between two points on a line, or in other words, the ratio of the altitude change to the horizontal distance between any two points on the line.
    a. Slope0
    b. Thing
    c. Undefined
    d. Undefined

123. The Gaussian _____ is an algorithm which can be used to determine the solutions of a system of linear equations, to find the rank of a matrix, and to calculate the inverse of an invertible square matrix.

Chapter 8. QUADRATIC EQUATIONS AND FUNCTIONS

a. Thing
b. Elimination method0
c. Undefined
d. Undefined

124. In mathematics and logic, a _____ proof is a way of showing the truth or falsehood of a given statement by a straightforward combination of established facts, usually existing lemmas and theorems, without making any further assumptions.
a. Thing
b. Direct0
c. Undefined
d. Undefined

125. _____ is the relationship between two variables, like a ratio in which the two quantities being compared are different units.
a. Direct variation0
b. Thing
c. Undefined
d. Undefined

126. The _____ governs the differentiation of products of differentiable functions.
a. Thing
b. Product rule0
c. Undefined
d. Undefined

127. In mathematics, a _____ is the end result of a division problem. It can also be expressed as the number of times the divisor divides into the dividend.
a. Quotient0
b. Thing
c. Undefined
d. Undefined

128. In mathematics, the term _____ is applied to certain functions. There are two common ways it is applied: these are related historically, but diverged somewhat during the twentieth century.
a. Thing
b. Functional0
c. Undefined
d. Undefined

129. The _____ is the professional licensure examination for architects in the United States and Canada.
a. Architect Registration Examination0
b. Thing
c. Undefined
d. Undefined

130. _____ is the art and science of designing buildings and structures.
a. Architecture0
b. Thing
c. Undefined
d. Undefined

131. _____, Greek for "knowledge of nature," is the branch of science concerned with the discovery and characterization of universal laws which govern matter, energy, space, and time.
a. Thing
b. Physics0
c. Undefined
d. Undefined

132. In mathematics, _____ geometry was the traditional name for the geometry of three-dimensional Euclidean space — for practical purposes the kind of space we live in.
a. Solid0
b. Thing
c. Undefined
d. Undefined

Chapter 9. CONIC SECTIONS

1. In Euclidean geometry, a _____ is the set of all points in a plane at a fixed distance, called the radius, from a given point, the center.
   - a. Thing
   - b. Circle0
   - c. Undefined
   - d. Undefined

2. In mathematics, an _____ .
   - a. Thing
   - b. Ellipse0
   - c. Undefined
   - d. Undefined

3. _____ systems represent systems whose behavior is not expressible as a sum of the behaviors of its descriptors.
   - a. Nonlinear0
   - b. Thing
   - c. Undefined
   - d. Undefined

4. A _____ represents a system whose behavior is not expressible as a sum of the behaviors of its descriptors.
   - a. Thing
   - b. Nonlinear system0
   - c. Undefined
   - d. Undefined

5. _____ are a set of equations containing multiple variables.
   - a. Systems of equations0
   - b. Thing
   - c. Undefined
   - d. Undefined

6. In mathematics, the _____ is a conic section generated by the intersection of a right circular conical surface and a plane parallel to a generating straight line of that surface. It can also be defined as locus of points in a plane which are equidistant from a given point.
   - a. Parabola0
   - b. Thing
   - c. Undefined
   - d. Undefined

7. In mathematics, a _____ is a type of conic section defined as the intersection between a right circular conical surface and a plane which cuts through both halves of the cone.
   - a. Hyperbola0
   - b. Thing
   - c. Undefined
   - d. Undefined

8. In mathematics, an _____ is a statement about the relative size or order of two objects.
   - a. Thing
   - b. Inequality0
   - c. Undefined
   - d. Undefined

9. In mathematics, a _____ section is a curve that can be formed by intersecting a cone with a plane.
   - a. Thing
   - b. Conic0
   - c. Undefined
   - d. Undefined

10. In mathematics, the concept of a _____ tries to capture the intuitive idea of a geometrical one-dimensional and continuous object. A simple example is the circle.
    - a. Curve0
    - b. Thing
    - c. Undefined
    - d. Undefined

11. In mathematics, _____ are the intuitive idea of a geometrical one-dimensional and continuous object.

Chapter 9. CONIC SECTIONS

   a. Thing   b. Curves0
   c. Undefined   d. Undefined

12. _____ is the middle point of a line segment.
   a. Thing   b. Midpoint0
   c. Undefined   d. Undefined

13. In geometry, the _____ of an object is a point in some sense in the middle of the object.
   a. Center0   b. Thing
   c. Undefined   d. Undefined

14. In classical geometry, a _____ of a circle or sphere is any line segment from its center to its boundary. By extension, the _____ of a circle or sphere is the length of any such segment. The _____ is half the diameter. In science and engineering the term _____ of curvature is commonly used as a synonym for _____.
   a. Thing   b. Radius0
   c. Undefined   d. Undefined

15. _____ is a three-dimensional geometric shape formed by straight lines through a fixed point vertex to the points of a fixed curve directrix.
   a. Right circular cone0   b. Thing
   c. Undefined   d. Undefined

16. In mathematics, a _____ is a two-dimensional manifold or surface that is perfectly flat.
   a. Plane0   b. Thing
   c. Undefined   d. Undefined

17. A _____ is a three-dimensional geometric shape formed by straight lines through a fixed point (vertex) to the points of a fixed curve (directrix)
   a. Concept   b. Cone0
   c. Undefined   d. Undefined

18. In mathematics, the _____ of two sets A and B is the set that contains all elements of A that also belong to B (or equivalently, all elements of B that also belong to A), but no other elements.
   a. Thing   b. Intersection0
   c. Undefined   d. Undefined

19. _____ is a test to determine if a relation or its graph is a function or not
   a. Vertical line test0   b. Thing
   c. Undefined   d. Undefined

20. Acid _____ ratio measures the ability of a company to use its near cash or quick assets to immediately extinguish its current liabilities.
   a. Test0   b. Thing
   c. Undefined   d. Undefined

21. The mathematical concept of a _____ expresses the intuitive idea of deterministic dependence between two quantities, one of which is viewed as primary and the other as secondary. A _____ then is a way to associate a unique output for each input of a specified type, for example, a real number or an element of a given set.
   a. Thing
   b. Function0
   c. Undefined
   d. Undefined

22. In geometry, a _____ is a special kind of point, usually a corner of a polygon, polyhedron, or higher dimensional polytope. In the geometry of curves a _____ is a point of where the first derivative of curvature is zero. In graph theory, a _____ is the fundamental unit out of which graphs are formed
   a. Vertex0
   b. Thing
   c. Undefined
   d. Undefined

23. _____ means "constancy", i.e. if something retains a certain feature even after we change a way of looking at it, then it is symmetric.
   a. Symmetry0
   b. Thing
   c. Undefined
   d. Undefined

24. An _____ is a straight line around which a geometric figure can be rotated.
   a. Axis0
   b. Thing
   c. Undefined
   d. Undefined

25. _____ of a two-dimensional figure is a line such that, if a perpendicular is constructed, any two points lying on the perpendicular at equal distances from the _____ are identical.
   a. Thing
   b. Axis of symmetry0
   c. Undefined
   d. Undefined

26. _____ is a notation for writing numbers that is often used by scientists and mathematicians to make it easier to write large and small numbers.
   a. Thing
   b. Scientific notation0
   c. Undefined
   d. Undefined

27. An _____ is a collection of two not necessarily distinct objects, one of which is distinguished as the first coordinate and the other as the second coordinate.
   a. Ordered pair0
   b. Thing
   c. Undefined
   d. Undefined

28. In plane geometry, a _____ is a polygon with four equal sides, four right angles, and parallel opposite sides. In algebra, the _____ of a number is that number multiplied by itself.
   a. Square0
   b. Thing
   c. Undefined
   d. Undefined

29. In mathematics, a _____ is a constant multiplicative factor of a certain object. The object can be such things as a variable, a vector, a function, etc. For example, the _____ of $9x^2$ is 9.
   a. Thing
   b. Coefficient0
   c. Undefined
   d. Undefined

Chapter 9. CONIC SECTIONS

30. The easiest _____ prime numbers resides in the use of the Sieve of Eratosthenes, an algorithm that discovers all prime numbers to a specified integer.
    a. Method for finding0
    b. Thing
    c. Undefined
    d. Undefined

31. A _____ is a set of numbers that designate location in a given reference system, such as x,y in a planar _____ system or an x,y,z in a three-dimensional _____ system.
    a. Thing
    b. Coordinate0
    c. Undefined
    d. Undefined

32. In mathematics and its applications, a _____ is a system for assigning an n-tuple of numbers or scalars to each point in an n-dimensional space.
    a. Concept
    b. Coordinate system0
    c. Undefined
    d. Undefined

33. _____ means of or relating to the French philosopher and mathematician Renã© Descartes.
    a. Thing
    b. Cartesian0
    c. Undefined
    d. Undefined

34. In mathematics, the _____ is used to determine each point uniquely in a plane through two numbers, usually called the x-coordinate and the y-coordinate of the point.
    a. Cartesian coordinate system0
    b. Thing
    c. Undefined
    d. Undefined

35. _____ is a relation in Euclidean geometry among the three sides of a right triangle.
    a. Thing
    b. Pythagorean Theorem0
    c. Undefined
    d. Undefined

36. In mathematics, a _____ is a statement that can be proved on the basis of explicitly stated or previously agreed assumptions.
    a. Theorem0
    b. Thing
    c. Undefined
    d. Undefined

37. The _____ of measurement are a globally standardized and modernized form of the metric system.
    a. Units0
    b. Thing
    c. Undefined
    d. Undefined

38. In geometry, a line _____ is a part of a line that is bounded by two end points, and contains every point on the line between its end points.
    a. Segment0
    b. Concept
    c. Undefined
    d. Undefined

39. In geometry, an _____ is a point at which a line segment or ray terminates.
    a. Endpoint0
    b. Thing
    c. Undefined
    d. Undefined

Chapter 9. CONIC SECTIONS

40. A _____ is a part of a line that is bounded by two end points, and contains every point on the line between its end points.
   a. Line segment0
   b. Thing
   c. Undefined
   d. Undefined

41. In mathematics, an _____, mean, or central tendency of a data set refers to a measure of the "middle" or "expected" value of the data set.
   a. Average0
   b. Concept
   c. Undefined
   d. Undefined

42. A _____ is a symbolic representation denoting a quantity or expression. It often represents an "unknown" quantity that has the potential to change.
   a. Variable0
   b. Thing
   c. Undefined
   d. Undefined

43. _____, either of the curved-bracket punctuation marks that together make a set of _____
   a. Parentheses0
   b. Thing
   c. Undefined
   d. Undefined

44. _____ is the practice of doing mathematical calculations using only the human brain, with no help from any computing devices.
   a. Concept
   b. Mental math0
   c. Undefined
   d. Undefined

45. A _____ is one of the basic shapes of geometry: a polygon with three vertices and three sides which are straight line segments.
   a. Triangle0
   b. Thing
   c. Undefined
   d. Undefined

46. A frame of _____ is a particular perspective from which the universe is observed.
   a. Thing
   b. Reference0
   c. Undefined
   d. Undefined

47. An _____ triange is a triangle with at least two sides of equal length.
   a. Thing
   b. Isosceles0
   c. Undefined
   d. Undefined

48. The metre (or _____, see spelling differences) is a measure of length. It is the basic unit of length in the metric system and in the International System of Units (SI), used around the world for general and scientific purposes.
   a. Concept
   b. Meter0
   c. Undefined
   d. Undefined

Chapter 9. CONIC SECTIONS

49. In geometry, a _____ (Greek words diairo = divide and metro = measure) of a circle is any straight line segment that passes through the centre and whose endpoints are on the circular boundary, or, in more modern usage, the length of such a line segment. When using the word in the more modern sense, one speaks of the _____ rather than a _____, because all diameters of a circle have the same length. This length is twice the radius. The _____ of a circle is also the longest chord that the circle has.
   a. Diameter0
   b. Thing
   c. Undefined
   d. Undefined

50. A _____ is the part of a fraction that tells how many equal parts make up a whole, and which is used in the name of the fraction: "halves", "thirds", "fourths" or "quarters", "fifths" and so on.
   a. Concept
   b. Denominator0
   c. Undefined
   d. Undefined

51. A _____ is the result of the addition of a set of numbers. The numbers may be natural numbers, complex numbers, matrices, or still more complicated objects. An infinite _____ is a subtle procedure known as a series.
   a. Thing
   b. Sum0
   c. Undefined
   d. Undefined

52. In mathematics and the mathematical sciences, a _____ is a fixed, but possibly unspecified, value. This is in contrast to a variable, which is not fixed.
   a. Constant0
   b. Thing
   c. Undefined
   d. Undefined

53. In geometry, the _____ are a pair of special points used in describing conic sections. The four types of conic sections are the circle, parabola, ellipse, and hyperbola.
   a. Foci0
   b. Thing
   c. Undefined
   d. Undefined

54. In mathematics, the _____ (or modulus) of a real number is its numerical value without regard to its sign.
   a. Absolute value0
   b. Thing
   c. Undefined
   d. Undefined

55. The _____ of a ring R is defined to be the smallest positive integer n such that $n\,a = 0$, for all a in R.
   a. Thing
   b. Characteristic0
   c. Undefined
   d. Undefined

56. In geometry, a _____ is defined as a quadrilateral where all four of its angles are right angles.
   a. Rectangle0
   b. Thing
   c. Undefined
   d. Undefined

57. An _____ is a straight line or curve A to which another curve B approaches closer and closer as one moves along it. As one moves along B, the space between it and the _____ A becomes smaller and smaller, and can in fact be made as small as one could wish by going far enough along. A curve may or may not touch or cross its _____. In fact, the curve may intersect the _____ an infinite number of times.

a. Thing
b. Asymptote0
c. Undefined
d. Undefined

58. A _____ can refer to a line joining two nonadjacent vertices of a polygon or polyhedron, or in some contexts any upward or downward sloping line. .
    a. Thing
    b. Diagonal0
    c. Undefined
    d. Undefined

59. A _____ is a function that assigns a number to subsets of a given set.
    a. Measure0
    b. Thing
    c. Undefined
    d. Undefined

60. _____ is a parameter associated with every conic section.
    a. Eccentricity0
    b. Thing
    c. Undefined
    d. Undefined

61. In physics, an _____ is the path that an object makes around another object while under the influence of a source of centripetal force, such as gravity.
    a. Orbit0
    b. Thing
    c. Undefined
    d. Undefined

62. A _____, as defined by the International Astronomical Union, is a celestial body orbiting a star or stellar remnant that is massive enough to be rounded by its own gravity, not massive enough to cause thermonuclear fusion in its core, and has cleared its neighboring region of planetesimals.
    a. Thing
    b. Planet0
    c. Undefined
    d. Undefined

63. In _____ algebra, a *-ring is an associative ring with an antilinear, antiautomorphism * : A ¨ A which is an involution.
    a. Thing
    b. Star0
    c. Undefined
    d. Undefined

64. An _____, also called a minor planet or planetoid, comes from a class of atsronomical objects.
    a. Asteroid0
    b. Thing
    c. Undefined
    d. Undefined

65. In the context of spaceflight, a _____ are any object which has been placed into orbit by human endeavor.
    a. Satellites0
    b. Thing
    c. Undefined
    d. Undefined

66. The Gaussian _____ is an algorithm which can be used to determine the solutions of a system of linear equations, to find the rank of a matrix, and to calculate the inverse of an invertible square matrix.
    a. Elimination method0
    b. Thing
    c. Undefined
    d. Undefined

67. The word _____ comes from the Latin word linearis, which means created by lines.

Chapter 9. CONIC SECTIONS

    a. Thing
    c. Undefined
    b. Linear0
    d. Undefined

68. A _____ is an equation in which each term is either a constant or the product of a constant times the first power of a variable.
    a. Linear equation0
    c. Undefined
    b. Thing
    d. Undefined

69. In mathematics, a _____ may be described informally as a number that can be given by an infinite decimal representation.
    a. Thing
    c. Undefined
    b. Real number0
    d. Undefined

70. The _____ is used to discard one of the variables in an equation, only to replace it with the actual value when solving multiple equations.
    a. Thing
    c. Undefined
    b. Substitution method0
    d. Undefined

71. _____ is the symbol used to indicate the nth root of a number
    a. Radical0
    c. Undefined
    b. Thing
    d. Undefined

72. A _____ is a negotiable instrument instructing a financial institution to pay a specific amount of a specific currency from a specific demand account held in the maker/depositor's name with that institution. Both the maker and payee may be natural persons or legal entities.
    a. Check0
    c. Undefined
    b. Thing
    d. Undefined

73. _____ are the basic objects of study in graph theory. Informally speaking, a graph is a set of objects called points, nodes, or vertices connected by links called lines or edges.
    a. Thing
    c. Undefined
    b. Graphs0
    d. Undefined

74. The _____ integers are all the integers from zero on upwards.
    a. Thing
    c. Undefined
    b. Nonnegative0
    d. Undefined

75. In mathematics, a _____ is the result of multiplying, or an expression that identifies factors to be multiplied.
    a. Thing
    c. Undefined
    b. Product0
    d. Undefined

76. _____ is the distance around a given two-dimensional object. As a general rule, the _____ of a polygon can always be calculated by adding all the length of the sides together. So, the formula for triangles is P = a + b + c, where a, b and c stand for each side of it. For quadrilaterals the equation is P = a + b + c + d. For equilateral polygons, P = na, where n is the number of sides and a is the side length.

Chapter 9. CONIC SECTIONS

a. Perimeter0
b. Thing
c. Undefined
d. Undefined

77. In mathematics, a _____ is a countable collection of open covers of a topological space that satisfies certain separation axioms.
   a. Development0
   b. Thing
   c. Undefined
   d. Undefined

78. In economics, supply and _____ describe market relations between prospective sellers and buyers of a good.
   a. Thing
   b. Demand0
   c. Undefined
   d. Undefined

79. In economics, economic _____ is simply a state of the world where economic forces are balanced and in the absence of external influences the values of economic variables will not change.
   a. Equilibrium0
   b. Thing
   c. Undefined
   d. Undefined

80. In economics, economic equilibrium is simply a state of the world where economic forces are balanced and in the absence of external influences the values of economic variables will not change. _____, for example, refers to a condition where a market price is established through competition such that the amount of goods or services sought by buyers is equal to the amount of goods or services produced by sellers
   a. Market equilibrium0
   b. Thing
   c. Undefined
   d. Undefined

81. In mathematics, a subset of Euclidean space R^n is called _____ if it is closed and bounded.
   a. Thing
   b. Compact0
   c. Undefined
   d. Undefined

82. In mathematics, _____ geometry was the traditional name for the geometry of three-dimensional Euclidean space — for practical purposes the kind of space we live in.
   a. Solid0
   b. Thing
   c. Undefined
   d. Undefined

83. A _____ is a set of possible values that a variable can take on in order to satisfy a given set of conditions, which may include equations and inequalities.
   a. Thing
   b. Solution set0
   c. Undefined
   d. Undefined

84. In common philosophical language, a proposition or _____, is the content of an assertion, that is, it is true-or-false and defined by the meaning of a particular piece of language.
   a. Concept
   b. Statement0
   c. Undefined
   d. Undefined

85. _____ is often used to describe the measurement of the steepness, incline, gradient, or grade of a straight line. The _____ is defined as the ratio of the "rise" divided by the "run" between two points on a line, or in other words, the ratio of the altitude change to the horizontal distance between any two points on the line.

Chapter 9. CONIC SECTIONS

    a. Thing
    b. Slope0
    c. Undefined
    d. Undefined

86. _____ is the study of determining the proper construction of bridges in accordance to the surrounding climate.
    a. Thing
    b. Bridge design0
    c. Undefined
    d. Undefined

87. In mathematics, the _____ f is the collection of all ordered pairs . In particular, graph means the graphical representation of this collection, in the form of a curve or surface, together with axes, etc. Graphing on a Cartesian plane is sometimes referred to as curve sketching.
    a. Graph of a function0
    b. Thing
    c. Undefined
    d. Undefined

88. In mathematics, the additive inverse, or _____ of a number n is the number that, when added to n, yields zero. The additive inverse of n is denoted −n. For example, 7 is −7, because 7 + (−7) = 0, and the additive inverse of −0.3 is 0.3, because −0.3 + 0.3 = 0.
    a. Opposite0
    b. Thing
    c. Undefined
    d. Undefined

89. In mathematics, the _____ of a coordinate system is the point where the axes of the system intersect.
    a. Origin0
    b. Thing
    c. Undefined
    d. Undefined

90. A _____ is an instrument used in geometry technical drawing and engineering/building to measure distances and/or to rule straight lines.
    a. Ruler0
    b. Thing
    c. Undefined
    d. Undefined

91. In mathematics, the _____ of a number n is the number that, when added to n, yields zero. The _____ of n is denoted −n. For example, 7 is −7, because 7 + (−7) = 0, and the _____ of −0.3 is 0.3, because −0.3 + 0.3 = 0.
    a. Additive inverse0
    b. Thing
    c. Undefined
    d. Undefined

92. In trigonometry, the _____ is a function defined as $\tan x = \sin x / \cos x$. The function is so-named because it can be defined as the length of a certain segment of a _____ (in the geometric sense) to the unit circle. In plane geometry, a line is _____ to a curve, at some point, if both line and curve pass through the point with the same direction.
    a. Thing
    b. Tangent0
    c. Undefined
    d. Undefined

93. _____ has two distinct but etymologically-related meanings: one in geometry and one in trigonometry.
    a. Tangent line0
    b. Thing
    c. Undefined
    d. Undefined

94. A _____ is the part of the dividend that is left over when the dividend is not evenly divisible by the divisor.

Chapter 9. CONIC SECTIONS

    a. Thing
    b. Remainder0
    c. Undefined
    d. Undefined

95. _____ in algebra is an application of polynomial long division.
    a. Remainder theorem0
    b. Thing
    c. Undefined
    d. Undefined

96. In mathematics, _____ allows the rapid division of any polynomial by a binomial of the form x − r. It was described by Paolo Ruffini in 1809. _____ is a special case of long division when the divisor is a linear factor.
    a. Thing
    b. Ruffini's rule0
    c. Undefined
    d. Undefined

97. In mathematics, a _____ is the end result of a division problem. It can also be expressed as the number of times the divisor divides into the dividend.
    a. Thing
    b. Quotient0
    c. Undefined
    d. Undefined

98. The _____ is a method of finding the derivative of a function that is the quotient of two other functions for which derivatives exist.
    a. Thing
    b. Quotient rule0
    c. Undefined
    d. Undefined

99. In mathematics, factorization (British English: factorisation) or factoring is the decomposition of an object (for example, a number, a polynomial, or a matrix) into a product of other objects, or _____, which when multiplied together give the original.
    a. Thing
    b. Factors0
    c. Undefined
    d. Undefined

100. In physics, a _____ may refer to the scalar _____ or to the vector _____.
    a. Potential0
    b. Thing
    c. Undefined
    d. Undefined

Chapter 10. EXPONENTIAL AND LOGARITHMIC FUNCTIONS

1. A _____ is the end result of a division problem.
   a. Quotient10
   b. -equivalence
   c. Undefined
   d. Undefined

2. A _____ is part of an answer to a question about why some object or process in a system has changed or was designed with some goal.
   a. Function10
   b. -equivalence
   c. Undefined
   d. Undefined

3. A _____ is a scheme for the numerical representation of the values of a variable. The interpretation we place upon the numbers of the _____, rather than the numbers themselves, makes the _____ useful. The most common scales are nominal, ordinal, interval
   a. -equivalence
   b. Scale10
   c. Undefined
   d. Undefined

4. A _____ is a well-defined collection of objects considered as a whole.
   a. Set10
   b. -equivalence
   c. Undefined
   d. Undefined

5. A collection of two objects such that one can be distinguished as the first element and the other as the second elemnt is an _____. An _____ with a as the first element and b as the second would be written as (a,b).
   a. Ordered pair10
   b. ADE classification
   c. Undefined
   d. Undefined

6. The x value of the point where the graph intersects the x-axis is the _____.
   a. -equivalence
   b. X-intercept10
   c. Undefined
   d. Undefined

7. An _____ is an indication of the value of an unknown quantity based on observed data. More formally, an _____ is the particular value of an estimator that is obtained from a particular sample of data and used to indicate the value of a parameter.
   a. ADE classification
   b. Estimate10
   c. Undefined
   d. Undefined

8. The very fact that we are measuring objects with respect to some characteristic implies that the objects differ in that characteristic; or stated in another way, that the characteristic can take on a number of different values. These properties or characteristics of an object that can assume two or more different values are referred to as a _____.
   a. Variable10
   b. -equivalence
   c. Undefined
   d. Undefined

9. A _____, also referred to as a universe, is any well-defined collection of things. By well-defined we mean that the members of the _____ are spelled out, or an unequivocal statement is made as to which things belong in it and which do not.
   a. -equivalence
   b. Population10
   c. Undefined
   d. Undefined

Chapter 10. EXPONENTIAL AND LOGARITHMIC FUNCTIONS

10. By _____ we mean collecting observations made upon our environment -- observations, which are the results of measurements using clocks, balances, measuring rods, counting operations, or other objectively defined measuring instruments or procedures. _____ may mean simply counting the number of times a particular property occurs.
   a. -equivalence
   b. Data10
   c. Undefined
   d. Undefined

11. The probability of correctly rejecting a false Ho is referred to as _____.
   a. Power10
   b. -equivalence
   c. Undefined
   d. Undefined

12. _____ is used synonymously for variable.
   a. Factor10
   b. -equivalence
   c. Undefined
   d. Undefined

13. A number that does not change in value in a given situation is a _____.
   a. Constant10
   b. -equivalence
   c. Undefined
   d. Undefined

14. An _____ is any process or study, which results in the collection of data, the outcome of which is unknown. In statistics, the term is usually restricted to situations in which the researcher has control over some of the conditions under which the _____ takes place.
   a. Experiment10
   b. ADE classification
   c. Undefined
   d. Undefined

15. _____ describes the phenomenon where the values of distribution tend to move towards the summary statistic. For example, values in a distribution tend to cluster about the mean, and in a linear _____ equation, they tend to cluster about the linear _____ equation.
   a. -equivalence
   b. Regression10
   c. Undefined
   d. Undefined

16. At times we must contend with variables that assume a large number of values. In this case it is typical to create _____ of values of the variable and then make a frequency tally of the number of observations falling within each interval. As is the case with any data reduction technique, detail is lost.
   a. ADE classification
   b. Intervals10
   c. Undefined
   d. Undefined

Chapter 11. SEQUENCES, SERIES, AND THE BINOMIAL THEOREM

1. A _____ is part of an answer to a question about why some object or process in a system has changed or was designed with some goal.
   - a. Function11
   - b. -equivalence
   - c. Undefined
   - d. Undefined

2. A _____, also referred to as a universe, is any well-defined collection of things. By well-defined we mean that the members of the _____ are spelled out, or an unequivocal statement is made as to which things belong in it and which do not.
   - a. Population11
   - b. -equivalence
   - c. Undefined
   - d. Undefined

3. A _____ is either a positive integer(1,2,3,...) or a non-negative integer(0,1,2,...).
   - a. Natural number11
   - b. -equivalence
   - c. Undefined
   - d. Undefined

4. A _____ is a well-defined collection of objects considered as a whole.
   - a. Set11
   - b. -equivalence
   - c. Undefined
   - d. Undefined

5. An _____ is an indication of the value of an unknown quantity based on observed data. More formally, an _____ is the particular value of an estimator that is obtained from a particular sample of data and used to indicate the value of a parameter.
   - a. ADE classification
   - b. Estimate11
   - c. Undefined
   - d. Undefined

6. A number that does not change in value in a given situation is a _____.
   - a. -equivalence
   - b. Constant11
   - c. Undefined
   - d. Undefined

7. A _____ is the relationship between two quantities.
   - a. -equivalence
   - b. Ratio11
   - c. Undefined
   - d. Undefined

8. An _____ is any process or study, which results in the collection of data, the outcome of which is unknown. In statistics, the term is usually restricted to situations in which the researcher has control over some of the conditions under which the _____ takes place.
   - a. Experiment11
   - b. ADE classification
   - c. Undefined
   - d. Undefined

9. The Greek letter _____ indicates summation.
   - a. Sigma11
   - b. -equivalence
   - c. Undefined
   - d. Undefined

10. _____ are any positive or negative number including zero.
    - a. ADE classification
    - b. Integers11
    - c. Undefined
    - d. Undefined

Chapter 11. SEQUENCES, SERIES, AND THE BINOMIAL THEOREM

11. A _____ is simply a polynomial with two terms.
    a. -equivalence
    b. Binomial11
    c. Undefined
    d. Undefined

12. A statement that can be proven true within some logical framework is a _____.
    a. -equivalence
    b. Theorem11
    c. Undefined
    d. Undefined

13. The probability of correctly rejecting a false Ho is referred to as _____.
    a. -equivalence
    b. Power11
    c. Undefined
    d. Undefined

14. The most important measure of central tendency, and one of the basic building blocks of all statistical analysis, is the arithmetic _____. It is simply the sum of all the set of values divided by the number of values involved. As a measure of central tendency, it is affected by extreme scores, and it assumes a ratio scale of measurement.
    a. -equivalence
    b. Mean11
    c. Undefined
    d. Undefined

15. A _____ is a subset or portion of a population. Samples are extremely important in the field of statistical analysis, since due to economic and practical constraints we usually cannot make measurements on every single member of the particular population.
    a. -equivalence
    b. Sample11
    c. Undefined
    d. Undefined

ANSWER KEY

Chapter 1
1. a	2. a	3. a	4. b	5. b	6. b	7. b	8. a	9. b	10. a
11. b	12. b	13. b	14. b	15. a	16. a	17. a	18. a	19. b	20. b
21. b	22. b	23. a	24. a	25. b	26. b	27. a	28. a	29. a	30. a
31. a	32. b	33. b	34. b	35. a	36. a	37. a	38. b	39. b	40. b
41. a	42. b	43. a	44. b	45. b	46. b	47. a	48. b	49. a	50. b
51. a	52. b	53. a	54. a	55. a	56. a	57. b	58. a	59. b	60. a
61. b	62. a	63. b	64. a	65. a	66. a	67. b	68. a	69. b	70. b
71. a	72. a	73. b	74. a	75. b	76. b	77. b	78. a	79. b	80. b
81. a	82. b	83. a	84. a	85. a	86. a	87. a	88. a	89. b	90. b
91. b	92. a	93. a	94. b	95. a	96. a	97. b	98. a	99. a	100. b
101. b	102. b	103. a	104. a	105. a	106. b	107. a	108. b	109. b	110. a
111. a	112. b	113. b	114. a	115. a	116. b	117. a	118. b	119. a	120. b
121. a									

Chapter 2
1. a	2. a	3. a	4. a	5. a	6. a	7. a	8. b	9. a	10. a
11. a	12. b	13. b	14. b	15. b	16. b	17. a	18. a	19. a	20. a
21. a	22. b	23. a	24. a	25. a	26. a	27. a	28. a	29. b	30. b
31. a	32. a	33. a	34. b	35. b	36. b	37. b	38. b	39. a	40. b
41. b	42. b	43. a	44. a	45. b	46. a	47. b	48. a	49. a	50. a
51. a	52. b	53. b	54. a	55. b	56. a	57. a	58. b	59. b	60. a
61. b	62. b	63. a	64. b	65. b	66. a	67. a	68. a	69. b	70. b
71. a	72. a	73. b	74. b	75. b	76. b	77. a	78. b	79. a	80. b
81. b	82. a	83. a	84. a	85. b	86. a	87. a	88. a	89. a	90. a
91. b	92. a	93. b	94. b	95. a	96. b	97. a	98. b	99. b	100. a
101. b	102. b	103. b	104. b	105. b	106. b	107. b	108. a	109. a	110. b
111. a	112. b	113. a	114. a	115. b	116. a	117. b	118. b	119. a	120. a
121. b	122. a	123. a	124. b	125. b	126. b	127. a	128. b	129. a	130. b
131. b	132. b	133. b	134. b	135. b	136. b	137. b	138. b	139. a	

Chapter 3
1. b	2. a	3. a	4. b	5. b	6. b	7. a	8. a	9. b	10. a
11. b	12. b	13. a	14. b	15. a	16. a	17. b	18. a	19. b	20. b
21. a	22. a	23. a	24. b	25. a	26. a	27. a	28. b	29. a	30. b
31. b	32. b	33. a	34. a	35. a	36. a	37. b	38. a	39. a	40. b
41. a	42. b	43. a	44. a	45. b	46. a	47. a	48. b	49. a	50. b
51. a	52. a	53. b	54. b	55. a	56. b	57. b	58. b	59. a	60. a
61. b	62. a	63. b	64. a	65. a	66. b	67. b	68. b	69. b	70. b
71. a	72. b	73. b	74. b	75. b	76. a	77. b	78. a	79. a	80. b
81. b	82. a	83. a	84. a	85. a	86. a	87. a	88. b	89. b	90. b
91. b	92. b	93. b	94. a	95. b	96. a	97. a	98. a	99. a	100. b
101. a	102. b	103. b	104. b	105. a	106. b	107. b	108. b	109. a	110. b
111. b	112. b								

Chapter 4

1. b	2. a	3. a	4. b	5. a	6. b	7. b	8. a	9. b	10. b
11. b	12. a	13. b	14. b	15. b	16. b	17. a	18. a	19. a	20. b
21. a	22. a	23. a	24. b	25. a	26. a	27. a	28. a	29. a	30. a
31. b	32. b	33. b	34. a	35. b	36. a	37. a	38. a	39. b	40. a
41. b	42. b	43. b	44. a	45. b	46. a	47. a	48. b	49. a	50. a
51. a	52. a	53. b	54. a	55. b	56. b	57. a	58. a	59. a	60. b
61. b	62. a	63. a	64. a	65. b	66. b	67. b	68. b	69. a	70. a
71. a	72. a	73. a	74. b	75. a	76. b	77. a	78. a	79. a	80. a
81. b	82. b	83. a	84. b	85. a	86. a	87. a	88. b	89. b	90. b
91. b	92. b	93. a	94. a	95. b	96. a	97. b	98. b	99. b	100. b
101. b	102. b								

Chapter 5

1. b	2. b	3. a	4. a	5. b	6. a	7. a	8. b	9. b	10. b
11. b	12. a	13. a	14. a	15. b	16. b	17. a	18. a	19. b	20. a
21. a	22. b	23. a	24. b	25. a	26. b	27. b	28. b	29. b	30. a
31. a	32. b	33. a	34. a	35. b	36. a	37. b	38. a	39. a	40. b
41. b	42. a	43. a	44. b	45. a	46. b	47. b	48. a	49. b	50. a
51. b	52. b	53. b	54. b	55. a	56. b	57. a	58. b	59. b	60. b
61. b	62. a	63. a	64. b	65. a	66. a	67. a	68. a	69. b	70. b
71. a	72. a	73. a	74. a	75. a	76. a	77. b	78. a	79. a	80. b
81. b	82. b	83. b	84. a	85. a	86. b	87. a	88. b	89. b	90. a
91. a	92. a	93. b	94. b	95. b	96. b	97. b	98. b	99. a	100. b
101. b	102. b	103. a	104. a	105. b	106. b	107. b	108. b	109. b	110. a
111. a	112. a	113. a	114. a	115. a	116. b	117. a	118. a	119. a	120. b
121. a	122. a	123. b	124. b	125. b	126. b	127. b	128. b	129. b	130. b
131. a	132. b	133. a	134. a	135. a	136. a	137. b	138. b	139. b	140. b
141. a	142. a	143. b	144. a	145. a	146. a	147. a	148. b		

ANSWER KEY

Chapter 6

1. b	2. a	3. b	4. a	5. a	6. a	7. a	8. b	9. a	10. b
11. b	12. b	13. a	14. a	15. b	16. a	17. b	18. a	19. b	20. a
21. a	22. a	23. b	24. a	25. b	26. a	27. b	28. b	29. b	30. a
31. a	32. a	33. a	34. a	35. b	36. a	37. b	38. b	39. a	40. b
41. a	42. b	43. a	44. b	45. a	46. b	47. b	48. a	49. a	50. a
51. a	52. b	53. a	54. a	55. b	56. b	57. b	58. b	59. a	60. b
61. b	62. a	63. a	64. b	65. b	66. a	67. a	68. a	69. a	70. a
71. a	72. a	73. b	74. b	75. a	76. a	77. b	78. a	79. b	80. a
81. b	82. b	83. a	84. b	85. a	86. b	87. a	88. b	89. b	90. b
91. a	92. a	93. a	94. b	95. a	96. a	97. b	98. b	99. a	100. b
101. a	102. b	103. b	104. b	105. b	106. b	107. a	108. b	109. a	110. a
111. a	112. a	113. a	114. b	115. b	116. b	117. a	118. a	119. a	120. b
121. b	122. a	123. b	124. b	125. b	126. b	127. a	128. a	129. b	130. b
131. b	132. a	133. a	134. a	135. b	136. a	137. a	138. b	139. b	140. a
141. a	142. b	143. b	144. a	145. a	146. a	147. a	148. a	149. b	

Chapter 7

1. a	2. b	3. a	4. b	5. b	6. b	7. b	8. b	9. b	10. a
11. a	12. b	13. a	14. a	15. a	16. a	17. b	18. a	19. b	20. a
21. b	22. a	23. b	24. a	25. a	26. b	27. a	28. a	29. b	30. b
31. b	32. b	33. a	34. a	35. b	36. b	37. b	38. a	39. b	40. b
41. a	42. b	43. a	44. a	45. b	46. a	47. b	48. a	49. a	50. a
51. a	52. b	53. b	54. a	55. a	56. b	57. b	58. b	59. b	60. b
61. a	62. b	63. b	64. a	65. b	66. a	67. b	68. a	69. a	70. b
71. b	72. b	73. a	74. b	75. a	76. a	77. b	78. a	79. b	80. a
81. a	82. a	83. a	84. a	85. b	86. b	87. b	88. b	89. a	90. a
91. b	92. a	93. a	94. a	95. a	96. b	97. b	98. b	99. a	100. a
101. a	102. a	103. b	104. b	105. a	106. b	107. b	108. a	109. a	110. b
111. b	112. a	113. b	114. a	115. b	116. b	117. b	118. b	119. a	120. b
121. b	122. b	123. b	124. b	125. b	126. a	127. b	128. b	129. a	130. a

Chapter 8

1. b	2. a	3. a	4. b	5. b	6. a	7. a	8. b	9. b	10. a
11. b	12. b	13. a	14. b	15. b	16. a	17. b	18. a	19. b	20. b
21. a	22. a	23. b	24. a	25. a	26. a	27. b	28. b	29. b	30. a
31. b	32. a	33. b	34. a	35. a	36. b	37. b	38. a	39. b	40. b
41. b	42. b	43. a	44. a	45. a	46. a	47. a	48. a	49. b	50. a
51. b	52. b	53. b	54. b	55. a	56. b	57. b	58. a	59. b	60. b
61. b	62. a	63. a	64. b	65. b	66. a	67. a	68. a	69. a	70. b
71. a	72. a	73. b	74. a	75. b	76. a	77. a	78. b	79. b	80. b
81. b	82. a	83. a	84. a	85. a	86. a	87. b	88. b	89. a	90. b
91. a	92. a	93. a	94. b	95. b	96. b	97. b	98. a	99. a	100. a
101. a	102. b	103. b	104. b	105. b	106. a	107. b	108. b	109. a	110. b
111. b	112. a	113. a	114. a	115. b	116. a	117. b	118. a	119. b	120. b
121. b	122. a	123. b	124. b	125. a	126. b	127. a	128. b	129. a	130. a
131. b	132. a								

Chapter 9

1. b	2. b	3. a	4. b	5. a	6. a	7. a	8. b	9. b	10. a
11. b	12. b	13. a	14. b	15. a	16. a	17. b	18. b	19. a	20. a
21. b	22. a	23. a	24. a	25. b	26. b	27. a	28. a	29. b	30. a
31. b	32. a	33. b	34. a	35. b	36. a	37. a	38. a	39. a	40. a
41. a	42. a	43. a	44. b	45. a	46. b	47. b	48. b	49. a	50. b
51. b	52. a	53. a	54. a	55. b	56. a	57. b	58. b	59. a	60. a
61. a	62. b	63. b	64. a	65. a	66. a	67. b	68. a	69. b	70. b
71. a	72. a	73. b	74. b	75. b	76. a	77. a	78. b	79. a	80. a
81. b	82. a	83. b	84. b	85. b	86. b	87. a	88. a	89. a	90. a
91. a	92. b	93. a	94. b	95. a	96. b	97. b	98. b	99. b	100. a

Chapter 10

1. a	2. a	3. b	4. a	5. a	6. b	7. b	8. a	9. b	10. b
11. a	12. a	13. a	14. a	15. b	16. b				

Chapter 11

1. a	2. a	3. a	4. a	5. b	6. b	7. b	8. a	9. a	10. b
11. b	12. b	13. b	14. b	15. b					

www.ingramcontent.com/pod-product-compliance
Lightning Source LLC
Chambersburg PA
CBHW082045230426
43670CB00016B/2783